Plastic
Tulips
in the
Winter

A Memoir

Plastic Tulips in the Winter

A Revised Memoir

By

DENICE VICKERS

Third Edition

First edition published in 2014. Revised edition published in 2020.

Cover design: Stephen Vickers [My son]

ISBN: 9781692537173

ISBN: 0988751003

ISBN 13:9780988751002

Library of Congress Control Number: 2012923747

Kindle Direct Publishing

Dedication

To my husband Steve, who I love, and under God, he is my breath.

To my children and their mates: Stacy, Brian, Misty, Stephen, Hillary, Denice, and Ben, I love being your mother.

To my grandchildren and their mates: Stacy, Tyrone, Sterling, Aleesha, Dylan, Misty, Navy, Cruise, Stephen, Roman, Liv, Hollyn, and my great-grandchildren, Declan, Anastasia, and Zora, you all have my heart.

To my sisters, Janice, and Leeann, and my brother Charlie, thank you for allowing me to open the pages of our life.

In memory of Cameron: Pam's son, who is dancing on the streets of gold. He loved this book.

In memory of Mom: whose hunger, and cry for God became deeply rooted in my own life.

In memory of Pam: my sister, my friend.

A NOTE FROM ME TO YOU

I would like to say a word to you before we begin this journey.

This book is written for you. I decided to write in a conversational tone.

If you have an open mind and are searching for answers to your life, please pull up a cushioned chair and footstool. Let me tell you about my life.

Would you like a cup of coffee or a glass of ice-cold sweet tea? Okay! Here we go...

Denice Vickers

1

Momma, Are We There Yet?

Summer 2007

ASHES TO ASHES, dust to dust, Momma always said she wanted a marching band with a choir singing, "When the Saints Go Marching In." She wanted it to be a time of celebration.

There Janice and I stood. She was sixty, and I was not far behind. Oh, where did the years go?

As Janice and I looked out over the ocean, the setting sun cast an orange hue across the water. All the sunbathers and the children playing had gone in for the evening. Our toes dug deep into the wet sand as the waves rushed over our feet. The breeze, filled with the salty air, blew against our faces. We stood side by side, looking in deep `silence..., and from the depth of my being, I heard my soul cry, "Momma, are we there yet?"

Summer 1955, Fifty-Two Years Earlier.

1

"Momma, are we there yet?" "Yes, Denice, now stop your wiggling. We will soon be there, and we are all going to have fun, Yay!"

Momma always said, "Yay!" It was her way of turning everything into a celebration.

Daddy was driving our 1954 four-door, two-tone, white, and teal Chevy Sedan. He had his usual pack of Winston cigarettes in his shirt pocket, with one lit in his hand. Dad's arm resting out the window wiggled his fingers as he let the wind pass through. His name was Charles Rady Perkins, a country boy who was six-two, thin, and very handsome. The men's Vitalis hair cream made his black, wavy curls look shiny.

Nellie May, my mom, was a city girl raised in Birmingham, Alabama. She sat in the front next to Daddy. She was five-two, had a small waist, shapely hips, large breasts, and beautiful legs that she liked to show off in her three-inch high heels. Her shoulder-length hair was thick, wavy, and auburn color. Her hourglass figure made her look like a Hollywood movie star. I don't believe she ever knew how beautiful she was. That day, she had on one of Daddy's starched white shirts, unbuttoned, with the sleeves rolled up.

Plastic Tulips in the Winter

Underneath was a one-piece leopard print bathing suit that tied behind her neck. She was barefooted.

My big sister, Janice Fay, was sitting by the window behind Daddy. The wind blew her hair back away from her face; she seemed to be daydreaming about her next adventure. She was eight years old, long, and lanky, with brown hair, brown eyes, and buck teeth.

Momma gave Janice a tight perm that made her hair look like she had put her finger in a light socket. Mom cut her bangs crooked. As she tried to straighten them out, the more corrupt, and shorter, they became. Her buck teeth, frizzy hair, her bangs, and glasses made her look weird in her school pictures.

Janice liked to stand on the stump in the front yard and sing opera to the passing cars. She was sure she could be a great opera singer. She asked Mom, "If I build a statue of myself, will it make me famous?" It made sense to us. Why not? Mom said that statues were of famous people.

Pamela Sue always sat in the middle playing with her doll. She was six years old and had long blonde soft curls that framed her face. Her dark brown eyes and dimples on both sides of her cheeks made her look like an angel.

Our maid, Bessie, said about Pam, "That child's dimples is so deep, I reckon the angels poked her there to make their marks and say to the world, that child's gonna be a girly girl."

Pam would say, "Hold me, Daddy, Hold me." Dad always swept her up in his lap.

I sat across the room, sucking my thumb, and wondered, "How does it feel to be held by daddy?"

My name is Denice Lynne Perkins, sitting behind Momma holding a little black Bible from Vacation Bible School. I'm four-and-a-half-years-old with dark brown eyes and jet-black hair cut in a pageboy. The freckles spread across my face like the stars in the sky.

Every summer, the sunburn on my shoulders got huge bubble blisters. Momma called it, that first good summer burn. We stayed brown as a biscuit for the rest of the summer.

I was an all-out tomboy and proud of it. My claim to fame was that I could burp loud, say a whole sentence in one long belch, spit the farthest, and I believed that I could whoop any boy's tail in the neighborhood. It was my routine every morning to find the fattest frog, put him in my pocket, and pull him out to speak to throughout the day.

Plastic Tulips in the Winter

Our home was Montgomery, Alabama— The Heart of Dixie. We could drive to Panama City Beach, Florida, in three hours, spend the day in the sun, and drive back that evening. It was always a blast.

Momma packed a picnic because she said it saved money. We had Golden Flake potato chips, peanut butter, and banana sandwiches on white Wonder Bread, and ice-cold sweet tea that tastes so good. Once we arrived at the beach, Momma laid out a blanket and started to unpack our picnic.

Daddy wore his white bathing suit and a white dress shirt, unbuttoned, with the sleeves rolled up to his elbows. He poured peroxide on his hair, and then took us aside, "Now, girls, don't call me Daddy today. Call me, Uncle Charlie."

"But why can't we call you, Daddy?" I asked.

"Hold your horses, Denice. We're going to play a game today: I'll walk up and down the beach and tell all the girls that I'm a lifeguard. I want to make sure that they feel safe while swimming."

I thought, "Daddy is brave to be a lifeguard today. I just didn't understand why I couldn't call him Daddy."

Mom was silent and let Dad do his thing rather than fight with him. She wanted the day to be about us. Mom spent the day playing in the water and building sandcastles in the sand.

As the sun went down, all that was left was the sound of the waves. She sat in the wet sand, stretched out her legs, and let the waves rush over her. With a calm look on her face, she turned toward me and softly spoke. "This is my favorite time of the day; I feel such peace." As she said the word peace, it seemed to stretch as it came out of her mouth, p-e-a-c-e. It was comforting and soothing to hear her say it. I would feel the emotion of her words, and the sweet sound of her voice as she said, "I feel such peace.

We waited for Daddy to find his way back to us.

2

A Cowgirl Or A Christian

THAT EVENING, WE stood in the kitchen around Mom as she prepared supper. She cooked fried pork chops, mashed potatoes, gravy, and lima beans that had been slow cooking all day. Every night, Momma's fresh homemade buttermilk biscuits completed the meal. She sliced up an onion and a tomato on a plate and placed it on the table. "Now, girls, eat you a slice of onion with your meal—it's good for your health." She reached for a piece of onion to chew on as she returned to the oven.

Momma's mother taught her how to make biscuits. Passing down recipes and style of cooking to your daughters was the Southern way. She took a big wooden dough bowl that her mother had given her, sat it on the counter, and began sifting flour and added Crisco and buttermilk to the mix. She kneaded the mixture in the wooden bowl until it made a ball, adding sifted flour until it felt just right. Smiling at us, she would say, "You don't want your biscuit ball to feel sticky, so you just keep adding flour."

Mom formed the biscuits in the palm of her hand, then placed them on a greased flat pan and into the oven. Within minutes, the aroma of fresh biscuits cooking filled the air as they began to rise.

She walked over to the sink, washed the dough off her hands, and suddenly broke into a song.

The love of God is greater far
  Than tongue or pen can ever tell.
  It goes beyond the highest star
  and reaches to the lowest hell.

O love of God, how rich, and pure!
How measureless, and strong!
It shall forevermore endure-
The saints' and angels' song.

There was peace as she sang. She picked up a fork and turned the pork chops that were frying in a large cast-iron skillet. Kicking her leg up in the air, she smiled, "That's my exercise."

The popping sound of the grease and the smell of the pork chops made you want dinner to hurry up, so you could sit down at Momma's spread. We loved just hanging around her.

"What do you girls want to be when you grow up? Y'all are so smart and beautiful. You can be anything you want to be, and go anywhere you want to go, just trust in God. God is the answer."

She looked at Janice, "Janice, what do you want to be when you grow up?" Janice gave a quick response, "Momma, I want to be a go-go dancer in a cage or a heart surgeon.

Let's look at this—two choices: A go-go dancer in a cage or a heart surgeon. That made sense to us, this was Janice, and it fit her. It was not unusual for her to get a frog or a turtle out of the ditch and cut it open to see how it works.

The three of us were still gathered around Momma, listening to each other's dreams. Momma asked, "Pam, what do you want to be when you grow up?"

With her hands pressed together to her cheek as if she was going to pray. "I want to be a singer and sing love songs like *Let Me Go, Lover and Love Is a Many Splendored Thing*. Pam was a romantic. Brenda Lee was one of her favorite singers; she sang, *Sweet Nothin's."* Pam would sit on the floor with her 45's, singing along playing her favorite love songs on the record player. The expression on her face was that of a child in love.

Then Momma asks, "Denice, what are your dreams?"

She took the pot of boiling potatoes over to the sink to drain them. I followed, "Momma, I want to be a cowgirl or a Christian." She wasn't surprised.

She held the lid to the pot and drained the potatoes. Her eyes lit up with delight. She smiled, "A cowgirl or a Christian, huh? Well, why can't you be both?"

Now let me tell you, Momma made us feel that what we had to say was important, and nothing we said was ridiculous. With all the emotion, that could be mustered up I said.

"Momma, if I'm going to be a real cowgirl, I'm going to have to kill me some Indians, and I don't think Christians can do that."

Looking at me, smiling from ear to ear, she threw her head back, shaking her thick hair, and laughed out loud, "Denice, you're a pistol-ball. You're right about that, but somehow, you'll find a way to be both. You, Denice, have gumption!"

Plastic Tulips in the Winter

Nodding in agreement, and not knowing what gumption was. I just knew I had it because Momma said so.

She placed the mashed potatoes down on the dinner 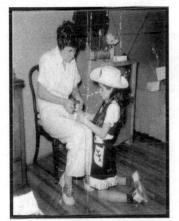 table next to the plate of pork chops. Janice pulled the hot biscuits out of the oven and put them on a plate next to the butter dish. Dinner was ready.

That night, lying in bed with the imagination of a child, wondering what it would be like to be a cowgirl, riding alongside Roy Rogers, and his horse Trigger. Oh, and Dale Evans, the best cowgirl ever, would be there, too. She was my hero! Visions of adventures as a cowgirl danced in my head, dreaming the sweet dreams of a child. Waking up to a day, no child should ever have to remember.

####

The next morning, Momma was dressed for work and making breakfast. Janice was pouring glasses of orange juice for everyone while Pam and I were sitting at the table coloring.

Daddy walked into the kitchen wearing his black dress pants, and a starched white shirt. As part of his usual routine, he said good morning to everyone, poured himself a cup of black coffee, and headed off to work.

Bessie, our maid, came in through the kitchen screen door, "Well, Mrs. Perkins, it's a mighty sunny day outside. It makes me want to get in my garden with my greens and cook me some up. "

I loved Bessie. She was a stout, full-figured black woman. Her grey hair pulled tight on her head in a bun, with her chubby arms wrapped around me as she drew close; her love swallowed me up into her big bosoms. She always called me her Baby Girl.

Momma grabbed her pocketbook and rushed out the door to her job as a bookkeeper. Janice and Pam finished eating and told Bessie they were going to their friend's house down the street.

Bessie said, "You stays here with me, Baby Girl. You just go outsides and play.

The sun beat down on my bare back as I searched for a frog in the ditch; it had the biggest frogs you've ever seen. There were broken Coca-Cola bottles in there and being barefooted made it hard to walk. Sitting

12

in the ditch, as if waiting for me, there was the perfect sized frog for today.

"Mr. Herbert, where have you been?" We were going to be buddies for the day. He liked the name too. He went straight into my pocket.

####

Around lunchtime, Daddy's car was in the driveway. I stepped inside and could hear the country music playing on the radio. Daddy was talking to someone. It was a woman's voice. I was standing by the door; they didn't see me, but I could see them. Daddy was sitting on our brown sofa.

It was our neighbor, Mrs. Marie, who lived a few doors down, standing barefooted with one knee propped up on the sofa next to him. She had short black hair and was wearing white short shorts and a royal blue button-up cotton shirt that tied in a knot under her breast. Laughing and teasing, she grabbed a throw pillow and held it to Daddy's face as if to smother him. As she stood up facing him, giggling with her legs slightly spread apart, and her hands on her hips. "Charlie, you stand up, and slow dance with me, you bad boy."

He grabbed her by the waist, pulled her down onto the sofa, and started to tickle her, "Sweetie, you got to go now, I have to get back to work. You're going to get me into some kinda trouble here." He laughed.

She giggled, "Oh, Charlie, stay a while longer."

####

Bessie cleaning the kitchen as I asked, "Bessie, why is that woman hugging on my daddy?"

Bessie's eyes opened wide, turning the whites of her eyes into a complete circle. She leaned down, and pushed the bangs away from my sweaty face, and whispered, "Lord have mercy, child. Now hush your mouth. You don't needs to be studyin' that. You go outside, and you play, I call you in when you lunch is ready."

She opened the screen door while giving a little push. "You stays outside until I call you in, you hear, Baby Girl?" "But..."

"No buts about it, you stay outside, and you waits for me."

It wasn't long, and Bessie opened the screen door, "Baby Girl, come on insides, and clean you self-up for lunch."

A sandwich was waiting. Bessie set the ironing board up in the living room. She said to me, "After you finish eaten, you come lays you self on the couch for you nap, and I am going to sing to you as I does my ironing, alright." Bessie began to sing.

Up in the morning,

Out on the job
I's work like's tha devil for my pay.
But that lucky ol' sun has nothin' to do
but roll around heaven all day.

It wasn't a black spiritual, but Bessie sang it like it was. Her voice had so much soul in it while she sang. I was lying there, sucking my thumb, picturing that lucky old sun just rolling around heaven all day.

FAT HENRIETTA

As I woke up from my nap, I could hear Pam giggling with someone in her bedroom. They were playing with her dolls, and what a surprise, she was playing with Fat Henrietta.

Now, you must understand why I called her Fat Henrietta. She was the neighborhood bully; if you had something she wanted; she took it. She knew, and we knew, just by sitting on top of one of us, you were a goner. She had frizzy brown hair, a red face as round as a basketball, freckles, and big lips that overtook her face. The voice that came out of that child sounded like angry thunder. She was meaner than a wet panther.

It was strange for Pam to be playing with her. Fat Henrietta saw me approaching them, and in her slow thunderous voice, yelled, "What do you want?"

I placed both hands on my hips to show her an attitude of my own, like, who's afraid of the Big Fat Henrietta? With my feet spread apart and standing firm. Having a deep alto voice of my own, knowing I too could sound like thunder. Gritting teeth and squinting eyes, "I'm going to play dolls with y'all."

Then, Fat Henrietta rose off the floor with her fist clenched at her side. She looked like a giant. She was as big around as she was tall, and twice my age. Her big red face began to turn redder, beat red; it looked like somebody was in trouble. Her response was that of a bear about to eat her live prey. "No, you're not! Get out of here!" she roared. Her words came out as if she had a mouth full of mush. What she was implying was, somebody was dead meat. Her face looked as if it were going to explode, and her tight fist ready to pound me into the ground or jerk me bald.

Plastic Tulips in the Winter

Pam jumped up from the floor and screamed, "Don't you dare hit my little sister!" For a moment, by the tone in Pam's voice, it sounded as if she was going to get rough.

But, being that I liked a good fight, and not waiting around to see if Pam had it in her. I swung at Fat Henrietta with legs, and arms, looking as if stomping on fire ants, and swatting bees all a while singing Elvis song, *"Hound Dog,"* all at the same time.

In my mind, I was going to beat her deader than a doornail. Singing, swinging, kicking, and hitting her as she was swung back, I was just about to belt out the next verse of *"Hound Dog,"* when she knocked me a good one across the face.

Now's my big chance to use my secret weapon. Pulling Mr. Herbert out of my pocket, and I threw him right in the center of fat Henrietta's face. Her eyes grew wide as she gasped for breath.

I doubled over laughing at the sight of that slimy frog's legs spread across Fat Henrietta's face and sliding down her cheek. I must admit it was a great site. I love that memory.

Immediately, she grabbed Mr. Herbert, and threw him across the room, and ran out the door screaming.

Running behind her, I yelled, "I'm going to tan your hide, you better run!" Watching my enemy run was a powerful feeling at that moment.

Our house was on a hill, and you could see her running and scream for a long way. She looked like a cannonball on fire.

Standing at the top of the hill, pounding my bare chest, and giving out a loud Tarzan yell, *"Ah-ah-AHHHH ah ah,"* knowing she could hear as she ran. I then yelled, "You're so dumb, if you threw yourself on the ground, you'd miss!" I loved the taste of victory, even at that age, and it never would change throughout my life.

Bessie had seen and heard it all. She was standing on the front porch watching my enemy run too, "My Lord's child, you make me laugh so hard, sometimes I think my stomachs gonna burst wide open like a watermelon. Girl, you are a wild child."

She just stood there with her hands on her hips, shaking her head as she laughed.

Plastic Tulips in the Winter

Looking back, realizing, God gives His children personality traits that are important for their journey. We still make our own choices along the way. Life has its way of forming and teaching us.

Janice was a born leader, a protector. She never felt inferior to anyone. Pam's soft, feminine traits were building, and creating the woman, she would become for His purpose. I will need a lot of fight standing in the gap spiritually for others, and myself, it was my destiny.

I HAVE LEARNED:

God gives His children personality traits that are necessary for their journey through life.

#PlasticTulips

I HAVE LEARNED:

We make our own choices along the way.

Our choices will determine our future.

The good news is, we can always correct our choices!

LIFE IS BEAUTIFUL THAT WAY

#PlasticTulips

3

Daddy's Killing Momma

IT WAS AROUND that time I had to stop putting frogs in my pocket. Bessie complained, "Mrs. Nellie, I's washed, and I's dries Denice's shorts, and as I folds them, I's found a dried up, dead, flat frog in her pocket. Miss Nellie, I just can't stands it. You got to do something with that child. It just ain't fittin for her to run around with frogs in her pockets." She then told Momma what I saw and heard with Dad and Mrs. Marie.

"Bessie, you can go on home. I'll finish up the ironing myself."

Bessie looked at the expression on Moms' face, "Mrs. Perkins, some men's folk are just old crackerjack fools." Then Bessie agitated, shaking her head, "My Lords, have mercy on his soul," as she grabbed her purse and walked out the door.

Mom changed into shorts and began to iron. A gentle breeze whispering through the open window caused the sheers to sweep against Mom's back. She says nothing but continues to push the iron back and forth with an expression of sorrow, and pain on her face.

Janice was sitting Indian style on the sofa watching TV as Pam combed her doll's hair, and I played with my plastic horse on the floor.

The front door opened; it was Dad coming home from work. Momma placed the iron down on the ironing board. She was ready to blast him. "What were you doing today with that woman?" Momma asked in an accusing tone.

"What do you mean, what was I doing? I was at work all day." He looked at her with disgust as he tightened his upper lip moving his head back, and forth almost spitting as he said, "You stupid woman."

Momma yelled, "Don't you look at me and lie to my face! I want to know what Marie was doing in our house. Who does she think she is coming to my house?" Momma's body trembled as she stepped closer to him.

His eyes narrowed as he clenched his jaw. Then slammed his car keys down on the table and yelled, "I don't know what you're talking about, you stupid woman. Nellie, you're just nuts. You're losing your mind, woman. You're going crazy. How do you get this junk in your head?"

She demanded an answer as she yelled, "Charles, what were you doing with her? Denice saw y'all, how could you?" I know you are having an affair with her. She has no business in my house, do you hear me?"

He walked over to the television to change the channel; it was his way of letting her know he couldn't care less. His lips curved up into a smirk, "You're always thinking the worst. What is wrong with you, woman? All I do is work hard and -come home to this."

Daddy looked at her, and tapped himself on the forehead, "You're the stupidest woman, always thinking crazy thoughts. What in the Sam Hill comes over you?"

The battle just increased with Mom's anger boiling over as she threw the hot iron at him, knocking the lamp off the table next to the sofa. Blasting him with her threats, "You tell her my children and my home are off-limits to her! She better never show her face around here. If I even see her talking to my girls, she will regret it."

Daddy put his hands around mom's throat, lifted her body off the floor, and then dropped her.

Mom screamed, "Charles, don't you touch me!"

He locked his jaw, and his nostrils began to flare as he took a step closer toward her. With his eyes narrowed, he slowly raised his hand in the air and slammed his open palm across her face. A red imprint of a giant hand began to form on the side of her cheek. She screamed out, "Don't you hit me, Charles!"

He grabbed her by the wrists, bent her arm behind her back, and threw her against the wall. All hell broke loose. He flung her to the floor, and around like a ragdoll. She was screaming for help, "Don't hit me, God help me, Oh, God, my children!"

Janice ran over and jerked me by one arm off the floor and onto the couch. She began to plead with Momma and Daddy to stop fighting. "Momma, Daddy, please stop."

Daddy was still man-handling her as she fought back. She jumped up from under him, ran into the kitchen, and came back, holding a butcher's knife.

Plastic Tulips in the Winter

Pam was in the corner with her knees to her chest, and her face buried into her baby doll, sobbing, saying, "No, Momma, no." Pam covered her eyes.

He folded his arms, and pushed out his chest as he blurted out, "Oh, what are you going to do now, stab me?" The smirk on his face said it all.

"If that's what it takes!" she yelled. Momma's hand went up in the air as she ran toward him with the knife and a blood-curdling scream. He grabbed her wrist, and they began to wrestle with the knife.

Janice jumped between them and tried to push them apart. She screamed, "Run, Denice, Run! Run to the neighbor's house! Tell them Daddy's killing Momma!"

I immediately ran through the kitchen, out the back-screen door, and into the cold, night, running as fast as my legs would carry me. My heart was beating out of my chest. I slid down into the ditch, crossing over into the neighbor's yard. Banging on their door, yelling, "Call the police!"

A man answered the door. Breathless, "Call the police, call the police! Tell them Daddy's killing my Momma!" Not for one second did I worry about Momma hurting Daddy.

The police came, but by the time they arrived, the fight had already stopped. The officer instructed them before leaving, "You two get your problems worked out, and keep it quiet." This would prove to be a regular event in our life.

While Bessie hung the clothes on the clothesline, I laid in the green grass, talking to her. I told her about the police coming to our house. I told her whatever was on my mind at that moment.

"Now you hush Baby Girl; you don't needs to talk about that." She changed the subject and talked to me about life. It was as if we were solving the world's problems under the clothesline every day.

4

Montgomery Bus Boycott

1955-1956

BESSIE APPROACHED MOM. She began to speak while she fumbled with a white sheet of paper rolled up in her hand.

Momma already knew what she was about to tell her. "Mrs. Perkins," Bessie began, "I needs to talk to you about something. I can't rides the bus tomorrow; I'm afraid I won't be able to comes to work.

There was a boycott in our town: a colored woman who worked in downtown Montgomery by the name of Rosa Parks refused to move to the back of the bus. The city ordinance it was required, to give up her seat to a white man. That Mrs. Parks had had enough of the treatment she and other coloreds received. She was arrested and put on trial.

"Bessie, don't you worry, I will drive my car, and pick you up."

Bessie responded, "Mrs. Perkins, I couldn't ask you to do that. You know those white folks won't like you giving me a ride in your car, and us black folks, we done join together, saying, we won't ride those buses till they treats us with respect. "

Mom said. "Bessie, you need the work, and besides, I need you." Bessie shook her head, "Thank you, Mrs. Perkins. I does need the work, and my Lord's lookin' out for me. You just come gets me at the corner of my street. Everything will be just fine. You know Mrs. Perkins, our tea is sweet, our days are long, and our faith is strong; God's gonna help us all." Mom shook her head in agreement with Bessie.

Momma loved Bessie and respected her as a hard-working woman. She told us Bessie had children of her own to feed, and she didn't need to stay out of work.

That night, while Momma was cooking supper, she told us, "It's wrong the way colored people are treated. It's not right. They're people just like us."

Janice responded, "Momma, Peggy Jo said her daddy told her that coloreds don't love their children, and they don't have souls that'll go to heaven. Is that true, Momma?"

I spoke up, and added, "Peggy Jo said that if a black person rubs up against you, their black color will rub off onto our white skin. I told Peggy Jo; Bessie's color don't rub off on me."

Momma bent down and looked us directly in the eyes. "Girls, you listen to me, and you listen to me good. Their blood is the same color as our blood. Why, if they got a cut on their arm, they'd bleed red blood just like us. They do have souls, and Jesus died for them, too. They love their children just as I love all of you. That Mrs. Parks shouldn't have to give up her seat to any man. She is a woman just like me, and it is wrong, and don't y'all ever forget it. God made us all the same. Don't listen to what people say, like Peggy Jo's father. You never listen to what others say, make up your own mind. What's important is what God says, and then what you say."

That same week Momma took us shopping downtown. Suddenly, we heard glass breaking. Momma quickly pulled us close to her for security without even checking to see what it was. "Oh, my lands," Momma expressed, as she faced the source of the noise.

"Lord, have mercy," the shopkeeper yelled as she ran to the front. "Someone threw a brick smack dab through the plate glass window!"

Momma's eyes revealed shock as she gathered us up like a mother hen would gather her baby chicks. "Come on girls. We need to get out of here."

With a sweeping movement, she grabbed my hand. "Janice, Pam, let's go now." Immediately, my arm flew out in front of me and jerked my body into motion toward the store entrance. Janice and Pam were walking swiftly behind us, trying to keep up the pace. "Mom, why did someone throw a brick through Miss Mitchell's window?" Janice asked.

"Hush, Janice, keep walking, we need to get to our car, and get home." It was strange, just a few seconds ago, we were picking out dresses, and now we were in the middle of a war zone. Nothing but panic, and yelling, screaming, stampeding, and terrible fear was in the air. Women were running with babies in their arms; children had started fleeing in every direction.

The smell of smoke filled the air as dozens of people were now running to their cars, trying to get away, while others were doing the vandalizing. Our hearts raced as Momma tried to get us to safety.

Plastic Tulips in the Winter

"Girls get in the car now and lock the doors." None of this was making sense to us, but we listened to Momma.

We were quickly in our seats with the doors locked as Momma pulled out of the parking spot, and cried out, "God, help us!"

Buildings and storefronts had broken windows with fires burning inside them. Cars and buses were also on fire and flipped upside down.

We had to drive slowly to keep from running over people in the street. Three white men were standing and yelling over a young black boy who was lying in the street. "I'll burn your black ass! Get your ass up, boy!" one shouted as he kicked him.

Another man yelled, "Boy, I'll shoot you graveyard dead if you don't get out of my sight!"

The young black boy took off, running down a dirt road in fear of his life. I hope he made it home safe. The police had fire hoses and were hosing people down, trying to stop the riot.

We drove a few blocks and came to a stop. Right in front of us, four white college-age boys began to rock a car back and forth, trying to flip it. The old black man was standing beside his car with his body shaking as he tried to protect his children. There were two young boys and a little girl about my age in the back seat. They had tears running down their faces, and their arms were wrapped around each other, holding tight so the white boys couldn't get them. Those boys were laughing at the frightened passengers and the old black man.

Momma jumped out of the car, holding up her hand, and yelled at the top of her lungs, "Don't you dare!"

They stopped what they were doing and looked up at Momma wide-eyed. They glanced left, right, and then at each other, before finally running off. She told the black man, "Mister, get your kids home to safety."

I was proud of my mother at that moment. Not that I wasn't proud of her before, but I think it just recalled what kind of person she was. She stood up for what was right for other people. Mom was always teaching us about our values. Reminding us, we belong to God. To respect and value ourselves and others. But, when it came to Dad hitting her and throwing her body around the room, she just put up with it; she didn't know her self-worth and value.

SUNDAYS

On Sundays, Dad always listened to the radio, gospel singers, and country music was his cup of tea. Hank Williams was one of his favorites. I sat on the sofa, sucking my thumb, watching Daddy slow dance with a broomstick around the living room, singing, *"Your cheatin heart will tell on you..."* He sang along with Hank as he swayed to the music. Hank sang, *"Hey, good lookin', whatcha got cookin'? How 'bout cookin' somethin' up with me?"*

He danced his way towards Momma, who was in the kitchen cooking. Grabbing her by the hand, with his other hand on her waist, danced her into the living room. He spun her around in her Capri pants.

Mom kicked her legs as she did the bop, still holding a wooden spoon in her hand. She was smiling and enjoying every minute of his attention. That was a good day, a good memory.

####

Dad, as always, was up to no good. For example, one day, I was in the back seat of our car as he was driving a neighbor around town and saying, "Yes, you see these two houses? I own over one hundred homes like them and rent them out."

He was a very convincing liar; he didn't need to lie; Mom and Dad were doing well together financially. I think Daddy lied so much that he believed his lies. Why, he could call a lizard an alligator, and believe it. What was odd is that other people believed him, too. We kids just listened to his words and continued to be kids. Summer was here, and we were going to have fun.

DIRTY, ROTTEN, SINNERS

It was a hot summer, Janice told Pam, and I, "Today we need to do something different. Why don't we have a church service in the garage?

Denice, you run around the neighborhood and tell all the kids to come to church, Pam, and I will set chairs out."

Momma always told me I had a built-in intercom system. So, I ran up and down the street, telling them about our service.

It wasn't long before the kids began to show up. Janice did the preaching, and Pam did the singing. I passed a paper plate around to take up the offering. No one had any money, but we still did it like a real church service.

Janice preached with a lot of enthusiasm, "Now, if any of you dirty, rotten sinners want to get saved from your dirty, rotten sin, then come down to the front, and repent. Repent from your ways right now." She shouted.

Pam standing on two stacked Coca Cola crates, was singing, *Let Me Go, Lover,* as loud as she could with her hands in the air. It wasn't a church song, but it was one of her favorite love songs.

Johnny, who was known to be a little slow, must have thought it was a real church. He ran to Janice, crying and slobbering all over her.

I think Janice got excited about her first soul to respond because she put her hand on Johnny's head, and yelled, "Get saved you dirty, rotten sinner! "We all clapped for Johnny; he was no longer a dirty, rotten sinner. I just believe God looked down on that poor boy and did something even if we were just kids.

I HAVE LEARNED:

God gives His children personality traits that are important for their journey through life.

#PlasticTulips

I HAVE LEARNED:

We still make our own choices along the way. Our choices can determine our future.
<u>*The good thing is*</u>*, we can always correct our choices!*

LIFE IS BEAUTIFUL THAT WAY.
#PlasticTulips

5

You Stupid, Stupid Woman

DADDY HAD WORK to do in Florala, Alabama. He took the family, so we could have a vacation for three days while he worked. He was a Royal Cup Coffee salesman; whose job was to keep all the A&P grocery stores stocked with coffee. Everybody liked him, especially the female cashiers. "Hey, Charlie," they would say in unison, with a giggle and a smile.

"Hey, pretty ladies. How is this lovely day treating you?"

He ran his fingers through his jet-black hair, giving them a wink and a smile. He was a charmer. He did this all so fluidly, like a dance, as he strutted to the sound of his own voice.

We checked into Nelson's Motel on Lake Jackson. The paint was peeling from the windowsills, but the room was clean and tidy. There was the primary kitchenette with yellow Formica counter, sink, small gas stove, and a refrigerator. It had a double bed and two single beds with quilts on them. The room had an odor like mothballs, and there was no air conditioning. We didn't care, because we were on vacation.

Mom had a cycling depression. When she was doing poorly, she was quiet. When she was better, what we called her good days, she laughed, danced in the house to the radio, cooked, and spent every breath telling us of her love for us.

Her mother told her about the love of God, but not about the power of God.

Mom did not know God could renew her mind. She didn't understand the crown of thorns was pressed down into the Son of God's head for her peace of mind. She didn't know He had come to make her the head and not the tail in life. Mom didn't realize God gives us knowledge through medicine to balance our brain hormones. She loved her children with every part of her being, but there was trouble in our home, and it was only a matter of time before the dam would break. God help us.

Plastic Tulips in the Winter

This day Janice noticed Mom was having one of her quiet days. "Look, Mom, isn't this going to be fun?" She tried to help Momma think happy thoughts.

Pam spoke up, "Momma, I promise it's gonna be fun." Pam and I started jumping up and down, looking in every nook and cranny of the motel room. We felt it was perfect.

Daddy looked at Janice, "I have to go to one of my stores to do some stocking; I'll be back at lunchtime."

Usually, Momma would be singing, and looking for her bathing suit, but she just didn't have the strength.

Janice, in her older sister's way, "Come on, let's get our swimming suits on, and go down to the lake so Momma can get some rest."

There was a big old oak tree with a thick rope hanging from one of its limbs. We took turns for about two hours, swinging out over the lake and letting go.

Janice looked up, "Pam, Denice, let's go, Daddy is back. I just heard him whistle for us to come to eat."

Letting go of the rope, I ran back up to the motel room, feeling very proud of my rope swinging accomplishments. I stepped into the room, to the familiar smell of propane gas.

Daddy ran to the bathroom and tried to open the door, but it was locked. He kicked the door until it broke off the doorjamb, he yelled, "Nellie, what have you done? You stupid, stupid woman!"

Mom was lying in a tub of water; her shorts and top were wet. Daddy was still yelling at her as she opened her eyes, moaned, and began rocking her head side to side, saying, "No, No, No."

Suddenly, all the fun of the morning vanished, and from inside of me came fear, and darkness. Daddy reached over to the space heater and turned off the gas. He jerked down the towels she had hung over the window and opened it to get fresh air into the room. He lifted her limp body out of the tub as he yelled again, "You stupid, stupid woman!"

He laid her on the floor. I noticed towels had been stuffed around the doorjamb to keep the gas in the room.

All Momma could do was moan, "No, No, No." She did not want to be rescued. Mom felt helpless, with no hope in sight. She was convinced death was the answer, and everyone would be better off without her. Oh, how wrong she was.

You might ask yourself, 'How could she do this to her children?' However, you would be thinking rationally, and at this point in her life, Momma could not think logically.

Daddy spoke, "Kids, let's pack up and go home; I'm going to put your Momma back into the hospital."

At times like this, I always got a knot in the pit of my stomach. It was a sense of having no control. I felt helpless and hated that feeling. These are the kinds of events in life that can either break or build us in our development and will take a work of God to heal the wounds. But GOD!

The psychiatrist put Momma on antidepressants and sleeping pills. She had had another nervous breakdown.

She had only been home for a few days when Daddy found her again in bed with pills spilled on the floor; she had overdosed on sleeping pills. He walked over to the bed, and began to shake her, yelling, "Woman, you stupid, stupid, woman. You're crazy as a nut case."

His words only backed up her feelings about herself. He picked up the phone and called an ambulance as he looked at us, "Your mother is nuttier than a fruit cake."

The ambulance arrived and pulled up our driveway with its lights flashing and siren blaring. The two ambulance drivers came running into the house and straight to Mom.

We watched as they wheeled Momma out of the house on a gurney. We followed them outside, watching as Mom gripped the sheet tightly under her chin and held her head to the side in shame, disgrace, and despair. They put her in the vehicle, and then shut the double doors on the back of the ambulance.

Daddy, eyes were like they were shooting fire, as he yelled, "This time, I hope you die!

The two ambulance drivers looked at Daddy and then each other. One guy was biting his lip as if he was holding back his tongue and wanted to beat the living hell out of Daddy. They got into the ambulance and drove away with Momma in the back.

I hated that she was alone, and hated Daddy for saying that to Momma. I always thought it was Daddy's fault Momma had these nerve problems. With Janice, Pam, and I all being born a year and a half apart from each other, Momma's mother passing away, and Daddy's lies and cheating.

I now know there were many reasons for Momma's undoing with an imbalance in her body. She just couldn't handle it all. She wanted death, but fortunately, death did not come.

YOU JUST DON'T KNOW

Daddy took us up to the hospital to see her. He stood at the nurses' station and instructed us to go into her room. I wanted Daddy to come with us, so I waited for a second, watching him.

He ran his fingers through his hair and walked up to the counter. "Hey, pretty ladies," with a smile, and swag.

"How are you pretty girls doing? Are the doctors treating y'all right today?" They were all smiles, shifting their hips in their white uniforms as they responded to his flirtatious remarks.

His eyes lit up when he talked to women. Daddy's tall and lean frame, black curly greased hair with one curl falling forward, melted them with excitement.

He leaned forward against the counter as he took a cigarette out of its pack, lit it, and held it to his lips, "So, what do y'all do on your time off?"

As they responded, Dad released the smoke from his lips, rolled the cigarette with the tips of his fingers, and then took another slow drag as he laughed at their answers.

I didn't care what they had to say; I just wanted him to come into the room. I looked back at him, one last time, and then followed Janice and Pam in.

A nurse followed us in, holding a clipboard in her hand, and chewing on a pencil as she read Mom's chart. She then looked up and flew off the handle at Mom. "How could you do this to your children!"

I looked at her, and thought, she wasn't just fat, she was mean too. Her ugliness was permanent. If she were an inch taller, she'd be round. I wanted to find a needle and pop that marshmallow woman.

Mom turned her face toward us, and muttered, "You just don't know." She moaned in her pain. "You just don't know; you just don't know. I'm so sorry; I'm so sorry, I'm so sorry, God, help my children."

Plastic Tulips in the Winter

Momma's face revealed an expression of fear and anguish. She lowered her chin and placed her hands over her face in shame at the nurses' harsh words.

She appeared aged and worn. With her head slumped sadly to one side, she cried out, "Oh, God help me."

The three of us just looked at her. I didn't understand why God did not help. The crumbling earth on the path of life was giving way under her steps, and we felt powerless to stop it. She heard voices that came from within her mind, saying, "You are worthless, give up, just die. Your children would be better off without you."

The voices that seemed to be inside her head were shouting so loud she couldn't hear the soft voice of God. Those were the thoughts that pulled her to the depth of despair.

She cried out, "God help me!" as she was sinking.

What Mom didn't realize was that God was watching, and He was listening. God heard her cries.

Doctors today might have diagnosed her with a chemical imbalance, such as bipolar disorder. To what degree, I'm not sure; I just know it was more than depression. Psychiatrists didn't have enough information back then, so if they thought that you were crazy, you were either put into a mental institution or diagnosed as depressed.

Mom received shock treatments many times. Shock treatments were electrical shocks to the brain. It seemed to help for a short while, but then she got depressed again.

We loved our Momma and told her everything was going to be all right.

Now that I'm grown, I wish that I could reach back in time to help that young woman and her little children. If I could, I would let her know that she is going to make it. I would tell her she is stronger than she realizes. She is a blessing to her children; they love her. And they will be blessed because of her strength. That God does care. God is watching. I would tell her; she always said God is the answer, and the answer is going to step into her, and her children's lives at an appointed moment in time.

It wasn't long after all this that Momma found out she was pregnant. Nine months later, she gave birth to my little sister, Leeann. I was nine years old and no longer the baby. She was our baby doll. She had curly, light brown hair and was born with a personality that lit up a room. As a little girl, Leeann loved dressing up in one of Momma's negligees, dragging it on the floor, and running around the house. We finished off her look with eye shadow, lipstick, and a string of feathers around her neck. She was our baby.

PAM, JANICE, AND ME

6

The Thin White Belt

W E HAD A COUSIN who was in his late twenties. He was in the military. He, his wife, and his three little girls would come into town from Birmingham to go to Gunter Air Force Base commissary. They came to visit several times that year.

Mom would get busy in the kitchen, cooking up a meal for all of us to eat together while Daddy turned on the stereo, laughing, and talking to our cousin's wife. She was pretty.

Us kids sat on the floor and played a board game, but our cousin would always speak up and say, "I'm going outside to swing, and I'm going to pick who will go with me."

He looked at Janice, Pam, and me, and would say, "I pick Pam because she is the most beautiful, and has the most beautiful blonde hair, and brown eyes."

Mom and Dad didn't notice she was leaving. Her blonde curls bounced as she was pulled away with his firm grip to her hand.

The expression on her face as she looked back at us was a look of regret for being picked. She looked sad; I didn't care that our cousin always picked Pam. I didn't want him to swing me anyway. I thought he was gross with his fat belly hanging over his thin white belt and his ugly white patent penny loafers that made him look as attractive as a wrinkled old man in a Speedo bathing suit.

That night, as Pam was combing her doll's hair, she told me, "It's not that good being beautiful, Denice."

I just thought she wanted to make sure my feelings weren't hurt. Thank goodness our cousin got transferred to a different base, and we didn't have to see his face again for years.

That year, Pam changed. She cried a lot and was afraid at night. The three of us slept in the same bed with Pam always in the middle. She took us through the same routine every night.

"Janice," Pam whispered, in her trembling voice, "Can I put my arm through your arm?"

"Yes, Pam." Pam sounded so scared.

Plastic Tulips in the Winter

"Denice, can I put my arm through your arm?"
I held my breath for a second, "Yes, Pam."

Again, she asked, "Janice, can I put my leg on top of your leg?" "Yes, Pam."

"Denice, can I put my leg on top of your leg?" And as always, I answered, "Yes, Pam."

She had both of her arms and legs wrapped on and through ours. That was how we slept so that Pam felt safe.

As we laid in the dark, all wrapped up with each other, Pam whispered, "I'm afraid."

I whispered back, "What are you afraid of?"

"I'm scared of being placed in a coffin and buried under the ground."

My stomach turned to ice when she said that.

I responded, "Don't think like that. You're scaring me."

She was wild with fear. "I'm scared of our cousin's white belt."

I whispered back, "Why are you afraid of a white belt?"

Janice spoke up, "Y'all' stop it, don't say that Pam. Let's go to sleep."

Some nights she didn't even ask, we just let her wrap herself around us.

That year was just not a good year for Pam. Her grades just dropped suddenly. She failed the third grade. On the last day of school, Janice walked in on Pam and found her crying in her bed. She was sobbing like her whole world was falling apart.

Janice sat on the edge of the bed. "What's wrong, Pam?" "I failed this school year, and everyone will know when I repeat the third grade. I don't want to go back to school next year. I don't want everybody pointing at me, saying I failed."

Janice put her arm around Pam, "I'm going to tell you a secret. If you do it, it will change your life." Janice always had good advice to give.

Pam looked up at Janice to hear the secret. "Pam, if you will act as if you're somebody, then everyone will think you are somebody." She continued, "Next year, just walk in that third-grade classroom, and act like it does not bother you one bit, and that you already know everything the other kids are going to learn that year. That's the way they will see you, as smart."

Pam, wiping the tears off her cheeks, looked at Janice, "Okay, I will." She trusted Janice and decided she would hold her head up high, act as if it did not bother her to repeat the third grade. You know what? It worked.

ROLLER-SKATING

On Friday nights, Mom would let us hook up with our friends at the roller-skating rink. We wore boy Levi jeans; there was no such thing as blue jeans for girls. We pegged them from the knee down to the ankle on the sewing machine. They were heavily starched and ironed with a seam down the front.

Pam always sat in the back seat between Janice and me, and of course, as was her routine, she would say, "Y'all hold me up. I don't want to wrinkle my pants."

She kept her legs straight, supporting herself on her elbows as we held her up, the drive to the skating rink. Janice and I were used to her perfectionism. Pam's hair, and make-up, for instance, always had to be perfect.

The skating rink was next to a black neighborhood that was called the projects. Black children stood watching the white kids go into the rink. I tried not to look over at them because one time I did, and my eyes came on a black girl about my age. She spoke up as our eyes met, "What's it like skating in there?"

I couldn't answer her, and I thought if I did, I would be bragging. I was ashamed I couldn't say, "Come in and see for yourself." Mom once spoke about this time we lived in, "Ignorance gone to seed."

DREAMING

We loved listening to all the latest songs. Elvis Presley had hit the scene, singing, *"That's All Right Momma."* He shook his hips and legs, which upset the adults. They said, "It's vulgar the way he shakes." Love songs and songs to dance to would play an essential role in our lives. He and others on the radio would take us through our teens, and help us forget our troubles, even if only for a moment.

Every Saturday morning, we danced in the living room to the television show, American Bandstand with Dick Clark as the host. We stood in front of the TV and screamed at our teen idols. It was cool viewing the bandstand teens dancing together. The hairstyles and clothes were important to us; we watched to see what styles looked best while dancing.

Janice and Pam's girlfriends slept over Saturday nights, and, of course, Janice was the life of the party. I would say she was a mixture of Carol Burnett, a comedian, and Ann Landers, a lady in the weekly newspaper that people wrote to for advice.

Plastic Tulips in the Winter

We listened on the record player to Pat Boone's *"April Love,"* Elvis Presley's *"Jailhouse Rock,"* The Platters' *"Smoke Gets in Your Eyes,"* Connie Francis' *"Where the Boys Are,"* and the Everly Brothers' *"All I Have to Do Is Dream."* Dreaming together was what we did, and boys were always the subjects of discussion.

CONFIDENCE

We were at a YMCA football game when Janice noticed that one of the teams didn't have cheerleaders. She had never been a cheerleader, but she decided to ask permission to form a squad and be the coach anyway.

They agreed, I guess, because her confidence made them think she could. We put up posters announcing tryouts, and over a hundred girls showed up. Pam and I became cheerleaders, along with ten other girls. Of course, it helped that Janice, our sister, was the judge for tryouts. We were already on the team, but Janice told us, "Y'all still have to try out."

My cheering looked more like a dance, with the swinging of the hips, not with the sharp moves required in cheerleading.

Janice gave them her confidence speech, "Now this is very important before you enter the field, you tell yourself, that all those people are waiting for you. The party can't get started until you arrive. You walk out on that field with an attitude of, I'm here. Let's party."

However, before our first game on a bet, that Janice would not jump into a ditch, which was about a ten-foot drop, she jumped. Now our Cheering coach, who didn't know cheers. Was hopping around on crutches with a cast on her broken leg.

We made up our cheers, and they had nothing to do with football. Here's my favorite one:

Bobbysocks

Knee socks

Nylon Hose

Sorry boys, that's as far as we go. Yay!

The other football team had cheerleaders with real uniforms, who knew real cheers, and had a real coach. At halftime, they marched out to the center of the field, swinging their ponytails, with matching ribbons in their hair.

We walked out as if we had a purpose with our homemade uniforms that Pam and Janice had designed and performed our cheer that had nothing to do with football. The boys on the sidelines cheered when we finished. We might not have had a store-bought uniform or knew real cheers about football, but we had

something the other girls didn't have, we had...
confidence.

FIRST KISS

Years past, and Pam was now in the sixth grade, and very popular. Valentine's Day, she received seven boxes of candy. She walked out of class, carrying all those boxes with her books. Her male teacher sang out loud Little Richard's song, *"The Girl Can't Help It."*

She was embarrassed to have so many boxes of candy. She saw me, and urged, "Denice, here, carry some of these."

"Okay, but you have to share."

As she handed me a few boxes of candy, she continued, "Mom said we could have a party tonight, so we've got to get home and get things ready."

A boy from Pam's class showed up, Tommy Vickers. All the boys had a crush on Pam, and Tommy was no exception. I thought he was the cutest boy I had ever seen. He had brown hair with bleach on the front with a flattop haircut.

As we drank our coke and ate popcorn, Janice, being the leader, "Now we are going to play spin the bottle." She began to explain the rules of the game.

Everyone sat on the floor, forming a circle, and then each took turns spinning the bottle, trying to make it spin fast. When the bottle stopped spinning, you and the person it pointed to would then go into Janice's bedroom to kiss one time.

It was Tommy Vickers turn next, so my eyes were focused on the bottle as it spun around and round until, finally, it came to a stop. It was pointing at me. I had never kissed a boy before.

It was my destiny. I'm going to be kissed by the most handsome boy in the room. I looked over at him; he crossed his arms and had a frown on his face. He wanted it to be Pam or some other girl. Not little, Denice, I didn't care. This was my moment to be kissed.

We walked into the darkroom, lit only by the soft glow of the streetlight shining in through the long, white, sheer curtains. My heart was pounding out of my chest.

Tommy walked over to the window and stood with his hands in his pockets, gazing out into the darkness. As I walked over to stand beside him, he turned as if to leave the room. Speaking up in a whisper, I asked, "Tommy, aren't you going to kiss me?"

"Yeah."

Plastic Tulips in the Winter

Then he kissed me. Yes, he kissed me. It was quick and to the point, but it was perfect; I felt as if I went straight to heaven. I followed Tommy as he turned to join the party.

The boys left, and the girls stayed for a pajama party. On the record player, Bobby Vee was singing one of my favorite songs, *Take Good Care of My Baby*.

With our baby-doll pajamas on, we lay across the bed, some girls on the floor, brushing and putting curlers in each other's hair. We tried on make-up as we reminisced about the night, and, of course, talking about boys. Our favorite Big Bam radio disk jockey played the latest tunes, and we danced the night away to songs like Dion's hit song, *Run Around Sue*.

My head was still in the clouds from my first kiss. I told the girls, "Tommy Vickers is the cutest boy in the world.'

Janice laughed, "Denice if you think Tommy Vickers is cute, you should see his brother, Steve Vickers." He was in junior high school with her.

I looked at her, "Oh no, no one could ever be as cute as Tommy."

Denice Vickers

What I didn't know then, was it would be Steve Vickers, who one day would take my breath away, and change my whole life.

7

Plastic Tulips

W E SOLD OUR HOUSE on the hill and bought a larger new home. It was a one-story brick house with green shutters and a front porch with four white columns. The living room had a big picture window, and the den was open to the kitchen.

Janice, being the oldest, got to have her bedroom. Pam and I shared a room with twin beds, but Pam never slept in her bed. She slept with Janice.

It was dead of winter on a Saturday morning. Daddy woke me, "Denice, get your coat on, and come outside." It was cold that morning, covered with frost, so damp and gloomy. I was all bundled up in my warm coat as Daddy handed me a handful of plastic tulips.

"Here, help me plant these tulips. Just push them in the ground."

Daddy bent over doing the same as we worked side by side, pushing every color plastic tulip into the ice-cold ground.

I asked, "Daddy, why are we planting plastic tulips in the winter?" I continued sticking them in the ground, waiting for his response.

"Because, Denice, as people drive by and see our tulips, they will wonder how we can grow tulips in the winter. You see, not everyone can do what we do. We will be the only ones that can grow tulips in the winter."

I remember thinking, "But these aren't real, they're plastic. Why would we try to trick people and make them believe we can grow tulips in the winter?"

It was odd to me even at that age, but it seemed to make sense to him. He was a great pretender, always trying to be somebody else, like a lifeguard on the beach, or a prominent real-estate owner, and now, growing plastic tulips in the winter. He would pretend to be many things in life, but never real. Dad was not mentally ill, just a great liar.

We didn't live very long in our new house; Momma and Daddy decided to rent it out. I didn't know why. I just knew we were moving. It seemed Daddy was becoming less interested in where we lived, so at that point, he only provided a roof over our heads. They bought a small, older home that was within walking distance to Capitol Heights Junior High and Robert E. Lee High School.

It was a one-story brick house with two bedrooms and one bath. The house had been painted white, but the white paint was chipping off, revealing the red brick underneath. We put our dining room table and hutch in the small breakfast area.

It wasn't long after we moved into the house that Momma found out she was pregnant again. Daddy told her to have an abortion, but that was out of the question for Momma. She gave birth to my brother, Charlie, named after Daddy. We had another baby doll.

At the same time, our neighbor on the hill, Marie, was also pregnant. It seemed we couldn't get away from that woman.

THE GREEN THREAD

The Police continued coming to our house with their blue lights flashing to break up the fights. Momma always screamed for Janice to call the Police. I think she was afraid that one day Daddy would kill her.

Mother's suspicions continued. She looked for evidence to prove those suspicions. Checking his collar for a lipstick smudge, the smell of perfume, or a number in his wallet. Maybe a receipt from a hotel. Mom did not shield us from the truth about Daddy. Unfaithful, a liar, a deceiver, a cheater, a womanizer, and a con artist were the words that kept Momma licking the ground with her mental wounds.

One night, after searching Daddy's car while he was out, she stormed into the house with a small green thread in her hand. It couldn't have been more than an inch and a half long.

I knew in her mind; it belonged to the other woman. Maybe, it came off her skirt, dress, or blouse while they were doing something they should not have been doing in the car. She was pacing the living room floor. Every few minutes, she looked out the window, lifting the side of the curtain. By the time he returned from the grocery store with his carton of cigarettes, she had worked herself into a frantic state. She stood with her arms crossed, holding the green thread, ready to let Dad have it. I thought, "Why did she have to find that green thread? It's just a piece of thread," but to her, it was more.

He walked through the door holding a bag. Mom throwing her hand up in front of his face, screamed, "What is this? What is this?"

Plastic Tulips in the Winter

I felt sick to my stomach as I stared at the green thread.

Daddy looked aggravated, "What in the Sam Hill do you think it is you fool? It's a green thread." He pushed her arm away as he walked past her and into the kitchen.

She followed him, screaming at the top of her lungs, "What was she doing in your car? I warned you to stay away from that tramp!"

Daddy turned around and backhanded her. Stunned, she stood there shortly with her hand on her face. Suddenly, she jumped at him, pounding her fists into his chest.

The next day, Momma had to go to work, and explain how she received her black eye, and bruises. No one got involved.

THE KKK

It was an uneasy time in the world, and change was coming, but not without agony. Our local newspaper, The Montgomery Advertiser, read like this, "An African American group called 'Freedom Riders' sparked a riot in downtown Montgomery. A crowd of white men, women, and children threw stones through the windows of the Negro First Baptist Church while

Dr. Martin Luther King, Jr., a black civil rights leader, and pastor of Dexter Avenue Baptist Church in Montgomery Alabama. was speaking." On August 28, 1963, that black preacher, Dr. King, delivered a speech, "I HAVE A DREAM" in Washington D.C.

That speech was persuasive. Children heard their parents talking about it. I heard it on television that night. I did not understand all that was said, and what would have to take place in the world for his dream to come true. I did recognize the right to have a dream, freedom, and that he wanted his four little children to live in a nation where they weren't judged by the color of their skin but the content of their character. That made sense to me. The Montgomery Advertiser reported Negro Freedom Riders were assaulted with clubs by a group of KKK as they arrived in Montgomery on their bus. On September 15, 1963, a bomb from a passing car blasted a crowded Negro church, the Sixteenth Street Baptist Church, killing four little black girls. Riots followed with two young Negro youth shot and killed. Gasoline being thrown into five businesses established by Negros and burned to the ground. It was an attack by the Ku Klux Klan.

Plastic Tulips in the Winter

Momma said the Ku Klux Klan was a bunch of rednecks filled with hate running around in white hooded robes.

Dad had gone to some KKK meetings. She told him he ought to be ashamed of going out in the woods at night, meeting with those rednecks.

Sitting in my seventh-grade class on November 22, 1963, the principal came over the loudspeaker, and announced, "The President of the United States has just been shot in Dallas, Texas as he, his wife Jackie, and the governor of Texas were riding in a convertible in the parade."

The kids in my class didn't know how to respond, most began to cry; others just walked down the halls quietly. The assassination was repeated over and over the TV. We sat in shock as Walter Cronkite reported the details.

Not long afterward, our school principal called for a meeting in the auditorium with the student body, teachers, and all. He walked up to the microphone, tapped on it a few times, and then began to speak. "Students, our school has been chosen to have two colored students join us this year. These two students are honor students and come from very stable homes. I expect you to be kind and respectful to them. They are not here to cause trouble; they just want to attend class, and I will not stand for troublemakers. Anyone who causes trouble will immediately be expelled from school. Is this understood?" Everyone responded, "Yes, sir."

"You may now go back to your classes." He walked away from the microphone, and no one was smiling; a few were whispering back and forth. It was not taken lightly.

The next day a Negro boy walked into my history class and took a seat. Some kids just didn't look at him, but I did. He was wearing a pair of dark jeans with a white tee-shirt and a dark blue jean jacket. His jacket had writing on it with a permanent black marker. Nothing terrible, just songs, and cool teen sayings. The main thing I noticed, on the front pocket of his jacket he wrote, Pocket of Love. I think he was trying to express that he was a teenager just like us. He noticed I was reading his jacket, so when our eyes met, I smiled, "Hey."

He laughed with a big smile, "Hey, back to you." I thought he was brave, and I hoped he felt he had a friend. I'm sure it was lonely at school for him, and the girl. Everyone pretended they weren't even there.

White teens didn't know what to say to a black teen. It was a time that understanding and knowing were all jacked up. Do they talk about the same things white teens do? Do they like the same music? Is there anything we would have in common?

Only a few had ever even talked to a black kid, just those white kids who lived on a farm and played with the children of the hired help. City kids had no contact with Blacks, except for the maids that worked in their homes.

Things were changing, life was changing, and it was shaping me.

Mom dancing while she cooked

Their choices determined their destiny.

8

Kick Him Out

ONE DAY JANICE and Pam came to me in my bedroom. I could tell they were up to something, "Denice, Pam, and I are going to tell Momma we don't want Daddy to live with us anymore. We want her to tell Daddy to leave. Are you coming with us to tell her?" I just tightened my upper lip and shook my head yes in agreement.

Momma came home from work before Daddy, and we did it. Janice looked at Mom and said, "Momma, we want you to raise us. We can have a happy home without Daddy. You have us, and we don't need him, he doesn't care about us. Momma, we want you to divorce Daddy. Kick him out."

Pam added, "We are teenagers, and it's embarrassing when the police cars come here with their blue lights flashing outside our house. We are tired of all the fighting."

I spoke up, "Momma, and we'll be happy with just you. It'll be all right."

Momma looked directly at us, and her mood was somber as she took a deep breath, exhaled, and asked, "Are y'all sure?" Although her face revealed a tired expression, there seemed to be a strength coming in her eyes as we spoke.

We all answered, "Yes, ma'am."

The torture of indecision and fear threatened to crush her all those years, but now her children were rising up with her to give her the strength to pull herself and her children out of the mess. We gave her a reason to live.

Finally, Mom chose to take control of her life. Her mind was made-up; it was the beginning of the battle being won.

At that moment, we heard Daddy's car pull into the driveway. Momma looked at us, and we at her. She straightened her back; it was she, and her children together, ready to face the storm. His car door shut, then the front door opened, and Daddy walked in. We stood beside Momma in the living room. She spoke calmly, and firm, "Charles, get your clothes and get out, it's over." There was strength in her voice that I had not heard in a long time.

His eyes stared in disbelief. He didn't even respond; he just walked into the bedroom and began to jerk the hangers from the closet.

Momma began to empty his drawers, throwing his clothes on the floor. Dad didn't say a word. It was apparent he wanted to go anyway. He took his clothes and walked out of our lives for good.

I was only ten years old at the time, but I felt the weight of the world lift from me as he walked out the door. It was a feeling of freedom. With him gone, there would be peace, laughter, and joy in our life. It would be just Mom and her five kids. I didn't give any thought of the fact when he walked out of our lives, so did his paycheck.

They had been married twenty-two years. Divorce was not easy, even if there were problems in the marriage, people stayed together. You either worked it out or remained unhappy. It was not a socially acceptable thing to do; only low-class people divorced. We didn't care. Her mind made up, and it was a battle won at that moment.

Momma had been telling Marie's husband about the affair with Daddy, but he didn't believe her. One night he called, "Nellie, do you think you could go with me? I think I see Marie and Charles' cars parked at a motel parking lot." That news wasn't a surprise, "Sure, I'll go with you."

It was them. Both divorces came quickly. Daddy, and his girlfriend, Marie, married. She gave up her two older children that were in elementary school, and she kept the baby. Finally, all of Momma's suspicions were confirmed. We could get on with our lives.

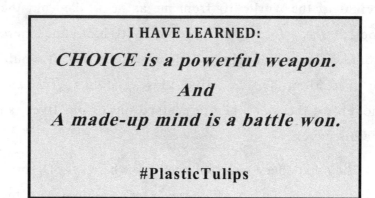

I HAVE LEARNED:

CHOICE is a powerful weapon.

And

A made-up mind is a battle won.

#PlasticTulips

Plastic Tulips in the Winter

A FATHERLESS CHILD

A fatherless child grows up thinking anything's possible, but nothing is safe. There was no longer a man in the house to do repairs.

I called Momma one day and asked her if I could take a crowbar and knock out a closet to enlarge the living room, and of course, she let me. I can't imagine letting one of my children do that, but it sure made me a do-it-yourself kind of person.

I learned to rig things at an early age. I learned that cardboard, taped over the window to cover up space where glass once was, helped block out the cold air. When a crack in our kitchen sink soon became a hole that was the size of a cereal bowl, I stuffed old rags in the hole to hold the water in the sink long enough to wash the dishes. A pot placed in the cabinet under the sink caught the water. Remembering to empty it was necessary.

I took the vacuum cleaner apart many times to repair it, but it eventually stopped working, so I had to sweep the carpet with a broom. The plastic knob to change the channels on the television broken off, so we rigged it with a dinner fork from the kitchen by bending the fork to wedge its teeth between the parts where the knob once fit. Some things that would be odd to others became standard to us.

The crazy thing was that our friends adjusted to our home as we did. If the fork went missing from the TV, he or she would say, "Where's the TV fork?" It would have been stuck back in the drawer with the other forks, but it was easy to spot. It was the bent one. Candles took the place of electricity if Mom couldn't pay the power bill that month.

We didn't have to apologize or explain any of these things to our friends; they just accepted whatever we accepted to be normal. That was a powerful lesson. I never felt ashamed of our situation at home.

Momma couldn't afford to buy meat, fruits, or vegetables. Coffee, bacon, eggs, biscuits, and gravy became our breakfast and dinner. We could eat a balanced lunch at school for thirty-five cents.

We saved the newspaper and stacked it by the toilet to replace toilet paper. Learning to rub the paper together to make it soft so it would flush was important.

At night, I could hear Momma's suffering, heartbreaking cry coming from her bedroom, "God, help me. Help me, God. Help me." I felt so bad for her; she seemed alone in her tears. Why didn't God help her? Did He know that she was calling out to Him for help?

Mom began to make declarations out loud for us to hear. With her right hand raised toward heaven, she would declare, "My children are a blessing, and are everything right in my life. God is a good God, and He is the answer. God will make way for my children, and me, I trust you, God."

Momma's declarations began to establish her foundation, pushing out the hopelessness. She was choosing to pay attention to the stones God laid in her path for her next step. She began to recognize the difference between the voices in her head, and the still small voice of God within. As she made these declarations, it began to stabilize her emotions. No one told her what the Bible says about the power of her tongue. And the power of her confession. The Holy Spirit was leading her, and she didn't even know it.

We felt safe and secure with Mom, no matter how hard things got. I guess Mom saw we needed her, and it made her stronger. Momma declared. "I would not give up my children for the world. My children are everything good in my life. If I had to beg, borrow, or steal to feed my children, I would do it."

She never asked for help, nor expected it from anyone but God. Not being lazy, working hard, and trusting God became her way of dealing with her depression. Mom would say to us, "If you're knocked down, you get back up. You get back up stronger, and you do what is right in the sight of God."

If I had to describe Mom in one word, it would be Strong.

We woke up each morning to the smell of coffee brewing, fresh buttermilk biscuits baking in the oven, and the popping sound of bacon frying in the black skillet. Momma would shout out singing, making the song sound like a military call.

> *Get up, get up*
>
> *Get up in the morning*
>
> *Oh, can't get them up,*
>
> *Oh, can't get them up*
>
> *Oh, can't get them up in the morning*

"Girls rise and shine. You don't want to be late for school. Breakfast is ready."

We were getting older, and, of course, we were typical teens, cutting, dyeing, and rolling each other's hair. We took our girlfriends' tubes of leftover lipstick that they were throwing away and made our own. We

Plastic Tulips in the Winter

were digging out the lipstick in the tube. We then put it on a stainless-steel soupspoon and held it over the fire of the top burner on the stove. We rolled an empty lipstick tube down and poured melted lipstick into it. Then we placed the tube on a plate in the refrigerator, standing it straight up. Once it dried solid, we had a new tube of lipstick. Mixing a little red and a little pink, we would come up with our shades.

It was an age for trying new things with friends. A girlfriend of mine named Susan smoked cigarettes. I tried one, and of course, Momma found out, and she beat the tar out of my legs. As she spanked me, she was crying out, "Dad-gum your hide, Denice, you are better than this. I won't have it; do you hear me? I won't have it; you are better than this."

I never smoked again, Momma's belief in my goodness, and me not wanting her to think less of me made me want to do right.

If a child is told they're no good, then why would anyone think they would turn out differently? The odds are against them already. Just think, if while she was spanking me, she was saying, "Your no good."

Momma's words were powerful in our lives, she said, I was better than that, and I believed her.

CHRISTMAS MORNING

Now that Daddy was gone, we didn't have the money to get a beautiful Christmas tree, but we learned that if you picked a cheaper one, with a bad side to it, and turned it toward the corner of the room, it worked just fine.

Our tree was always falling over, and even though we rigged it with a string to the curtain rod, it still fell. Momma just laughed, "It wouldn't be Christmas if the tree didn't fall."

Christmas morning, we woke up to the smell of turkey cooking in the oven and Krispy Kreme donuts for breakfast. Our friends began showing up as early as they could to get away from their own homes.

Momma was in the kitchen singing, cooking, making her dressing, and fruit salad. Everyone knew that at our house, you were welcome for Christmas lunch. She always wanted us to be free spirits and did not believe in putting on airs. "Beauty is only skin deep, but ugly goes clean to the bone. "She would remind us.

She sat listening and watching us as we acted out our stories, laughing along with us. Mom talked to us about seeing people for who they were and not who they portrayed themselves to be. We were to have mercy on people, being kind, and not judgmental. The most valuable lesson she gave us was to know who you are and to like yourself as a person.

Mom gave us another gift without knowing it. I call it a gift of self-expression. She communicated with us and wanted to hear our thoughts on any subject. She would share her thoughts and let us all have our own opinions.

We were not corrected but directed. We were never too silly or too loud when we spoke. Mom always threw in, "Her two cents worth."

We all laughed at the other's latest adventures late into the night, and Momma kept a fresh pot of coffee always ready. She made sure any teenager that walked through our doors felt welcome, and that she was a listening ear for them. It was mostly boys between the ages of sixteen to twenty years old showing up. They always said they wished they could talk to their parents the way we all spoke to Mom.

Janice was in the tenth grade at Lee High School. Pam and I were in the seventh and eighth grades at Capitol Heights Junior High School. Leeann and Charlie were three and five.

Momma had so many responsibilities as a single parent with five children.

The courts told Dad he had to pay twenty-five dollars a month for child support. That was five dollars per child for a month. He never paid it.

MISS CHARMING

We settled into the school year and lived for the weekends. I was always thinking of boys or what fun I was going to have for the coming weekend.

As I was sitting in my math class, the speaker made a loud squeaking sound, and the school secretary, in her high-pitched slow southern voice, "Miss Durham, could you please send Denice Perkins over to the gym. Mrs. Hogan wants to talk with her."

Miss Durham stopped in the middle of her sentence, "Denice, take your books with you just in case the bell rings while you are there."

I walked in Mrs. Hogan's office, and, to my surprise, there sat Pam. Mrs. Hogan smiled at me, "Denice, take a seat."

Pam had a look of fear on her face. She didn't know what was going on and was sitting all proper.

I plopped myself down in the chair next to her. I was sure there was nothing to worry about because Mrs. Hogan was always a friend to the students.

Plastic Tulips in the Winter

She spoke, "Pam, and Denice, I am going to tell you something, but it cannot leave this room."

There was a moment of silence as we sat side-by-side, waiting for her next words. "The student body voted for seventh, eighth, and ninth grade Miss Charming this morning. They will walk out on the field Friday night at the football game and presented."

She stared at us for a second, gave us a smile, "Pam, Denice, you were both voted as Miss Charming at your grade level. However, we are unable to let y'all have it due to your grades. You must have a B average; therefore, the runner-up will be announced as the winners. They must never know that you won. Normally we do not give out this information, girls, but I felt you two girls should understand why it is essential you pull your grades up. I trust you not to repeat this, for it would rob the other girls that are going to be announced this afternoon as Miss Charming."

We were speechless. It didn't seem fair, and everybody knows that whoever gets it is considered the most popular girl in that grade.

She then asked, "Girls, do we understand each other?" "Yes, ma'am," we both responded.

"You can go back to your classes now."

Walking out of the gym toward the front door of the school, Pam buried her face in her hands as we walked. Tears were running down her cheeks as she tried to wipe them away before we went back to class.

I wanted to comfort her, "Pam, what's important is we know. Look at us, Miss Charming," I did a little spin. Pam was still wiping away, her tears.

"Denice, you just don't get it, we didn't win. It just seems we can't have anything."

I responded, "But Pam, they voted for us, that's all that matters, as for me, I'm Miss Charming."

She quickly said, "Well, not to me, I want to walk out and have the roses placed in my hands by the most popular boy in the class."

For a moment, I pictured me with my crown on, and the handsome boy handing me my red roses, with the crowd standing and clapping. Sometimes life just isn't fair. But then I quickly chose to look on the bright side.

"Pam, I will go congratulate the winner after she is crowned Miss Charming. As I look at that crown on her head, I will stare at it and say to myself; she is borrowing my crown." Foot, the way I thought was, what matters, is I knew the truth. It just rolled off my shoulders, but Pam took it to heart.

Plastic Tulips in the Winter

She pulled her grades up and made homecoming queen the next year in the ninth grade. That seemed to smooth out the feeling she had of things just never working out for her. A fatherless child feels the rug can be pulled out from under their feet at any moment. Therefore, life goes on. That was the year I met Robin.

I HAVE LEARNED:

A fatherless child feels the rug can be pulled out from under their feet at any moment.

#PlasticTulips

I HAVE LEARNED:

A fatherless child feels,

Anything Is possible,

BUT Nothing is safe.

#PlasticTulips

BUT

I HAVE LEARNED:

GOD IS A FATHER

TO THE FATHERLESS

#PlasticTulips

9

Carpenter's Dream

1964

A S I WAS CUTTING the front yard in shorts, and barefooted, Robin walked by. I recognized her from school. With her hands on her hips, "I can't believe my eyes, Denice Perkins is cutting the grass."

I turned the lawnmower off, wiping the sweat off my forehead with my T-shirt, and replied, "Well, Robin, it's like this—if I don't do it, it won't get done. You're looking at the chief cook, and the bottle washer, I have to do it all."

Robin lived around the corner in some apartments with her mom, who was divorced. She was tall like me, thin, and had boxy hips. I say boxy because she didn't have a rear-end. Her honey-colored blonde hair had streaks in it short in a bob style. Her big blue eyes were as blue as the ocean, along with a big bright smile.

She didn't know what it was like to have a yard with grass to cut, "It looks like fun. Can I try it?"

My first thought was, this girl is plum crazy. I stepped away from the lawnmower, "Sure, knock yourself out." I went into the house, fixed me a glass of ice-cold sweet tea in a mason jar. I sat on the step of the front porch, watching her cut our grass. Isn't that funny, well I mean, funny because what was fun to her, was a responsibility to me.

Robin and I became best friends. We were inseparable. Robin's friend, KT, also began to hang out with us. KT had a silky, vanilla-colored shoulder-length hair, green eyes with a pretty face. Her smile was slightly crooked; her skin was tan and smooth like butter. KT had the biggest boobs I had ever seen on a girl my age. I always thought she was chubby, now that I think about it, she was not fat; it was just those huge boobs.

Robin beat her boobs, and yelled to the top of her lungs, "Grow, Grow," it didn't work. I told her if she continued to hit them, she would stunt them for sure.

KT told us, "Rub them with cocoa butter."

I knew all the cocoa butter in the world was not going to make mine grow. I ordered a gadget from a magazine; I think the inventor's name was Mark. It was a pink plastic gadget. It looked like a pair of false teeth, the size of our hands, and it had a thick spring in the middle. You put it between the palms of your hands, elbows out, and up, and then squeeze your hands together repeatedly. The magazine article read, "Guaranteed to increase your bust two sizes in a matter of weeks."

Robin and I did it every day while chanting, "I must, I must, I must increase my bust," it didn't work. It just made our armpits sore. We called it Mark. Eventually, we gave up on Mark. I threw it in the trash.

Every day, we walked home from school together, and the same two boys would check us out when we passed them. I guess Jimmy got tired of us ignoring him, so this day, he yelled out, "Denice Perkins is a carpenter's dream, flat as aboard."

That did it; he was dead meat. I was hot mad; I was going to be ready for him the next time I saw him. I swear that boy made me angry. I wasn't allowed to swear, but now I'm almost seventy telling you about this, and I guess I've earned this moment in time to swear. Dadgum, yes, I said it, mom said that's slang.

The plan came to me as I was eating a two-cent piece of hard candy named Mary Jane. Mary Jane would be the name to use since we didn't know anybody at school by that name.

Well, as fate would make it happen, the very next day, we passed each other, and the loudmouth began to yell, "Denice Perkins is a carpenter's dream, flat as a board," that was all I needed.

I swung around, looked that loudmouth straight in the face, and with my finger pointed at him, and I yelled, "Jimmy Port, everybody is talking about you, and Mary Jane. I defended you, but if you don't shut your big fat mouth, tomorrow I'm going to get on the school intercom system. I'll tell the whole school that you and Mary Jane did do what they're all talking about."

His face turned pale white as he began to stutter, "Whoa, whoa, what do you mean? Who is Mary Jane? What are they all saying?"

Squinting my face, shaking my head, "Jimmy, you know who I'm talking about. You know what you did with her. Boy, you better walk softly because I have my eyes on you. If you call me a carpenter's dream one more time, I'll stop protecting you, and you'll wish you had me on your side. Jimmy, you mess with me, and I'll fry your fish."

"Wait a minute, Denice, tell everybody it's not true.

Plastic Tulips in the Winter

I didn't do anything with Mary Jane."

With fire coming out of my eyes, and a warning to Jimmy, I replied, "It's looking dreadful for you. I'll do my best to stop all the talking, but boy, you better walk softly and stay on my good side. Remember this, Jimmy: I'm the mouth of the South, and all I need is an intercom."

That took care of Jimmy, anyway, how could he know I was a carpenter's dream. I wore the most padded bra JC Penny's sold.

Robin, KT, and I made an excellent trio. Robin confessed she never kissed a boy, and I knew KT hadn't either. Neither one of them had dated. We had fun talking girl talk, and I just absolutely knew that Robin needed to get over her fear of kissing. I didn't have a lot of experience—only the kiss from Tommy Vickers the night we played spin-the-bottle. That kiss lasted for three years. I was sure that one kiss had made me a seasoned veteran.

We were planning on going to a dance, and I knew a boy was going to give us a ride home. I instructed Robin, "When he walks us to the door, I'm going to go straight in, leaving you with him.

If he starts to kiss you, don't panic. "I gave my best advice, just put your lips together, and close your eyes, and wait."

Everything happened just as we planned. I walked into the house, turned the radio up loud, and began to do the twist in the living room to Chubby Checker's "Let's Twist Again."

I sang along, knowing Robin was getting her first kiss. Robin came running in, jumping up, and down with excitement and joined me doing the Twist.

PIERCED EARS

Pierced ears were the latest fad, but there wasn't anywhere to have it done in Montgomery unless you went to a tattoo parlor. I wanted my ears pierced, but we didn't have the money to do that.

Pam assured me she could do it. The radio was on, and the Beatles, *"Shout"* was playing. Which was perfect because we were shouting. She took an ice cube out of an ice tray and held it tightly on my ear as I grit my teeth. All the while, she was screaming as she stuck the needle through my earlobe.

I yelled out, "Pam, stop you're screaming!" Hyperventilating, like she couldn't breathe, she bent over at her waist to catch her breath. "Aww, I can't do the other one, I just can't." She began to jump around like a chicken with its head cut off, screaming and laughing.

With the needle still hanging out of my earlobe, I yelled, "Pam, don't you do this, you can't quit on me now."

She was screaming while rolling around on the bed, acting like she was in pain, but it was my ear. "No, I can't, I can't do the other one."

I told her, "I can't walk around with one pierced ear. I'll hold an ice cube on the other ear, and you pull that needle out and put the earring in."

She calmed down, sat up, fanned her face with her hands, "Okay, here it goes."

Pam pulled the needle out and then continued to yell the whole time she was pushing the earring post through my ice-cold ear lobe. I was the one in pain, but she was doing enough screaming for the both of us, my ears were pierced.

Pam had enjoyed it so much she did Janice's.

Janice and I both held Pam down to pierce her ears. We all screamed at the same time.

MOMS' NERVES

MOMS' nerves seemed better since Daddy was out of the house, or she was just trying hard for us. She had a hysterectomy and was taking hormone pills, which helped her. Maybe she had a hormone imbalance or a chemical imbalance her whole life. Who knows? Back then, doctors didn't even make the connection.

During dinner, Mom always brought up the topic of Daddy, and Marie, and what they did to us. I would get a knot in the pit of my stomach. I didn't want to hear it, but it was always on her mind. We tried to lift her spirits by making her laugh and changing the subject.

The psychiatrist told Mom, "Nellie, it's like you have this pain, and you keep it in your pocket. You pull it out every day and rehearse the hurt repeatedly. You need to pull it out and throw it away, once and for all."

He was right, but that was hard for her to hear. He also told her that she took life too seriously. I guess it's hard not to be so serious when you are the only provider for five kids.

Daddy only called once, it was on a Friday, "Denice, tomorrow I'll pick you, Leeann, and Charlie, up, and take yawl out for ice cream."

I got Leeann, and Charlie ready, and we sat, and waited all day, but he never showed up. I never looked for or expected anything from him again.

PRETTY THINGS

My friend Donnie from school invited me over for dinner with his family. He lived on the same street where I heard Daddy, and his new wife Marie lived. I went to Dad's house and knocked on the door. It was a brand-new neighborhood.

Marie answered it, "Hey, Denice." She was in short-shorts and was barefooted. "Is Dad home?"

She responded, "Come on in, I'll get him for you." She walked with a bounce like she didn't have a care in the world. "Charles, it's Denice, she's come to see ya."

While waiting on Daddy, I scan the room to see all the pretty things. They had all new furniture, a sofa with two shiny wooden end tables, and a matching coffee table with matching lamps that sat on each table. There was an oil painting hanging above the sofa and a green leather recliner for Daddy. I also noticed a brand-new stereo cabinet that had a record player and radio combined. A silk flower arrangement sat on top of the stereo. Above the color television were two brass wall sconces that held pale peach silk flowers.

Daddy walked in with a big grin on his face. He was barefooted and bare-chested with his white shorts. "Hey."

I smiled to hide my nervousness, "I was over here in the neighborhood and thought I would just drop by and visit for a minute."

"Well, have a seat. Marie, get Denice a glass of sweet tea."

Daddy had his gospel quartet music playing on his record player. "I just wanted to say hey. I'm having dinner with a friend of mine in the neighborhood. I knew you lived here, and just wanted to see you. I can't stay."

He responded, "No, stay a while and visit."

I felt uncomfortable and wanted to leave. I guess you could say I was upset seeing all the pretty things. I told Dad, "I better go." I left.

Walking back to Donnie's house, I had the thought, "Everything at our home was broken-down, nothing matched, not even the dishes matched.

But one thing I knew, I would not want to live with them if my life depended on it. I would rather be with Momma and struggle. I would rather eat eggs every day of my life and continue wiping my rear end with newspapers than leave my Mom."

I knew, in the lonely nights, Mom's very soul was crying out to God for help for her and her children.

Plastic Tulips in the Winter

I never told Momma that I went to see him that day. I knew it would hurt her to know about the new house, and all the pretty things, and Marie not having a care in the world. It was as if she had the world by its tail.

I couldn't change that I was his child, but I was proud to say, "I am my mother's daughter."

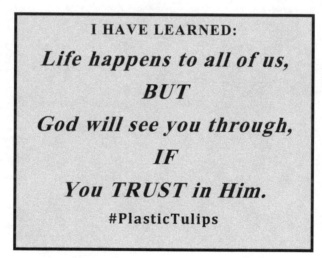

I HAVE LEARNED:

Life happens to all of us,

BUT

God will see you through,

IF

You TRUST in Him.

#PlasticTulips

10

Life Happens

WHEN JANICE BECAME a teenager, her favorite clothes to wear to parties were what we called the "shimmy dress." It was a white strapless dress with layers of little string tassels all over it. She wore her hair chin length with bangs. Her black, cat-eye shaped rhinestone glasses were the latest in fashion. Janice could shimmy, and go-go the night away, she just never got her cage. Oh, wait a minute... I take that back. In the future, she does get to dance in a cage.

She and Mitchell were always together. When you saw Janice, you saw Mitchell; they never wanted to be apart.

One day Janice went to Mom; she wanted to get married. In Alabama, two sixteen-year-olds could not marry, but in the state of Mississippi, if each teenager had one parent's permission, they could legally marry.

Momma, and Mitchell's dad, Harris, a divorcee, took the two teens to Mississippi to get married. Mom and Harris talked and enjoyed each other's company during the three-hour trip and three-hour drive home. They began dating, and it was not long before they were married.

We were excited. She needed to feel loved by a man. Harris was tall with broad shoulders, dark eyes, and black wavy hair. He was a good man, a gentleman.

Harris was a recovering alcoholic. She knew nothing about alcoholics, and not long after the wedding, he started back to his drinking. He moved into a boarding house so that we would not see him drunk.

Moms' father passed away and left Mom some money. It was not a lot, but it was enough to pay for rehab for six weeks; enough time to get Harris dried out. Mom took the rest of the money and rented office space for her, and Harris to open an accounting firm since Harris had an accounting background, just like her. However, he just never showed up for work, and Momma lost her entire investment.

Harris wanted to stay dry. We didn't know how to Help him.

Plastic Tulips in the Winter

PAM

In the meantime, Pam was now dating William, who was four years older and played bass guitar in a popular local band. William was six feet tall and blonde. Girls liked boys in rock bands, and Pam was no exception. I had never seen her head over heels crazy over any boy before, but she was with this one.

His band played every weekend at various locations in town, and college campuses nearby. Within a few months, Pam walked into the kitchen "Momma, I'm quitting school, and marrying William, he has signed up with the Navy."

Of course, at school, all the cliques were buzzing, and I knew what they were whispering. I begged Pam, "Please don't get married, please."

My speech was, "Well, Janice might have gotten married, and now you, but I'm telling you, I'm not going to get married until I'm at least twenty-one."

In the South, during that time, if you weren't married in your twenties, you were called an old maid.

Pam stared straight at me as she spoke, "Denice, you're going to eat those words. You're going to fall in love, and you'll want to get married, too."

Momma was not happy about it, but she saw in Pam the same determination Janice had had.

William was twenty years old, and Pam was only sixteen. They could get married with the consent of one parent of the teen, so Momma, Pam, and William went down to the courthouse, and they got married.

Pam wore a two-piece cream-colored suit with a pair of cream high heels. Momma bought Pam flowers to hold in her hands.

At this time in the South, girls married right out of high school, unless they were going to college. We were living at a time when our young boys weren't given a choice but sent off to the Vietnam war. People felt that if they were old enough to fight on the battlefield, they were old enough to be married. They married the girl they loved before they left to fight a war.

PERSONALITY REHAB

In school, it was a requirement that everyone takes physical education. We were all in the gym, lined up in rows with white T-shirts, and our red PE shorts.

Our teacher was facing the front with her back to the class, leading us in exercises. I was always playing around, wanting to have fun. As she led us in jumping jacks, I led the class in dance moves—the *Twist,* the *Monkey*, and the *Jerk.*

They all followed me as she was facing forward and thought we were following her. She turned around and caught me right when I was doing my best moves.

"Denice, Robin, I think the principal would love to discuss the subject of leadership with you, and how the paddle feels on your behind." She pointed toward the gym doors, "Go to the office." At that moment, I knew I was about to enter personality rehab.

I felt terrible that Robin was getting punished with me for something I started. We sat in the office waiting for the principal when the office phone rang, and the secretary answered it. Robin and I sat there whispering back, and forth, conspiring on how we were going to explain to the principal.

The secretary put the phone on hold, walked over to the school microphone system, and pushed a button on the gym speaker. I looked up from Robin to hear her say, "Please send Denice Perkins to the office."

I thought, "Did she just call my name?" I cleared my throat and spoke up. "I'm right here."

She looked surprised to see me sitting there. "Denice step into the principal's office. There is a phone call for you. It's your mom." I turned to Robin, "Uh-oh, they've called my mom!"

I picked up the phone, "Hey, Momma."

There was a moment of silence. Then, in a solemn voice, "It's your daddy... He's dead. I'll be there in a minute to pick you up."

I stepped out of the office and told Robin. She put her arm around my shoulder to comfort me. I wasn't crying, but I was a little shocked by the news.

While standing in front of the school waiting for Momma, I tried to decide who I wanted it to be. I knew I liked Harris, but his alcohol problem had just made life harder for us. Daddy only shows up now and then with a different woman to show off and to remind us kids that we're no good. We heard Daddy, and Marie had gotten a divorce. The affair lasted for years, but the marriage lasted one year.

Well frankly, I wasn't sure which one I wanted to be dead, as Momma drove up; I got in the car, and asked, "Momma, who's dead, Harris or Daddy?"

"It's Harris, I decided to go check on him at the boarding house. He didn't answer the door, so I looked through his bedroom window, and saw him lying in bed. I knocked on the window, but he didn't wake up.

Plastic Tulips in the Winter

The boarding house manager let me in, Harris was sleeping on his side, covered up with his blanket as always. He looked like he was sleeping, but he was gone."

The autopsy indicated he died from a combination of alcohol and sleeping pills; it was an accidental overdose. They had been married for about a year when he passed. One thing I realized is that death happens, and life goes on.

"MUSTANG SALLY"

Janice's marriage didn't last but about two years, and then she found herself divorced, and with a baby boy. Men were always attracted to Janice because she was miss personality. She was always up to something, always pushing the limits and still the leader of the pack. Janice said she felt like the black sheep of us girls, but she wasn't. She just had a wild hair. Janice, later in life, would be diagnosed with Bipolar Disorder. We would come to learn that this condition is genetically passed down from a parent. Looking back, it did explain some of her actions.

The song *"Mustang Sally"* was popular on the radio. Janice and her new man had a red Mustang. She had a way of making men believe in themselves, so her husband did very well while he was married to her. Janice was always coming up with business ideas.

MOMMA

Momma made a choice every day to be happy and not feel depressed. In the coming years, I would learn that choice is a powerful weapon. The Bible states, "As a man thinks in his heart, so is he" (Proverbs 23:7). Deuteronomy says, "This day I call heaven, and Earth as witnesses against you that I have set before your life, and death, blessings, and curses. Now choose life and blessing so that you and your children may live."

No one is defeated until he gives up. I will say now, looking back, I wish mom had stayed on antidepressants, it would have helped her, and it would have been easier on us kids.

As an adult, I realize that a woman can go through hormone deficiency. Your brain has hormones, it is supposed to put out, but if it doesn't, medication can help. They can replace the hormones your body is lacking. People deal with so many deficiencies that God has given the medical field the knowledge for.

There is no shame in needing help. If your body is not producing serotonin or estrogen, for example, then why not try obtaining it through medication?

Plastic Tulips in the Winter

Now doctors are finding out about thyroid deficiency and its effect on the body. Life could have been different, but just as I say that, I feel my life has had a purpose.

What we now know is that laughter changes our brain chemicals. The Bible says, "Laughter is a medicine." Life is beautiful. Life is funny. Heck, people are funny. Sit in a park, and people watch. You will have a good laugh, by just people watching.

I HAVE LEARNED:

You have four significant chemicals in your brain. They influence our happiness, and each plays a different role in happiness. Together these chemicals create a balance.

1. Dopamine   3. Serotonin

2. Oxytocin   4. Endorphins

1. Dopamine: is involved more with anticipation than the actual "happiness" feeling, described as a striving emotion.

2. Oxytocin: It makes us feel empathy that helps us feel close and bonded to others when it's released.

3. Serotonin: If you're in a good mood, you've got serotonin to thank. Besides, if you're in a bad mood, you can blame the {lack] of serotonin.

4. Endorphins: Mask pain or discomfort. When it comes to designing happiness, endorphins help you "power through."

Are there anyone of these chemicals you feel you are lacking? Copy this page and get help. God will lead you to the right specialist. An Endocrinologist specialize in glands, hormones and metabolism.

#PLASTICTULIPS

Plastic Tulips in the Winter

COLLEGE

College was never an option for us, and in the future, I will mix and mingle with highly educated people and be impressed with their accomplishments but never feel inferior.

Confidence in one's self goes a lot further than knowledge, not in an arrogant way but a realistic and secure way. It can only come with experience and training, although a good ego helps.

The knowledge I can get, but self-confidence, you must put on from within. It's a decision, a choice.

Momma taught us the meaning of life, and it was instilled so deep within us. Life has its way of forming who we are and who we become.

Some of the most educated people I have met swim in shallow waters. Education is excellent if you have that opportunity. It should never replace integrity, manners, kindness, and love toward people. It is a mistake to believe that wealth and fame can equate with intelligence. I listen to some people talk and notice that what they talk about are things they have head knowledge and book knowledge but have never proven true in their own life.

Life teaches us some hard lessons; it is a great teacher. It will be your teacher if you will be its student. Life is Beautiful that way.

LIFE IS PASSING ME BY

One evening, Momma and I were sitting having a cup of coffee. "Mom, life is going to pass me by. I think I want to start dating boys and not need to be in love with them. I'm going to start dating boys just for friendship. I have decided I will date boys, and not wait to look for that perfect guy. I just can't find a guy that knocks me off my feet."

Mom smiled, "You should just get out there and date. Have fun, Denice. Life is short. Your young, and you need to enjoy your teens."

I began to go on dates with every boy who asked, just for fun. Matthew was one of them who was tall, slim, tanned, with brown eyes and black hair. He was a Hollywood gorgeous guy.

We started dating, he had all the good manners a girl could want, and he sure wasn't hard on the eyes.

We laughed and talked about everything. We ran with the same group of friends and knew many of the same people. After about the fifth date, he kissed me.

Plastic Tulips in the Winter

I knew it was going to happen, and I had already decided ahead of time to let him. I wanted to see if I felt any electricity.

My first and the only kiss had been years before when I played spin the bottle with Tommy Vickers, and it took a long time to get my head out of the clouds, but, to my disappointment, kissing Matthew was like kissing a wall. I did not feel anything. I didn't know what kind of guy it was going to take to knock me off my feet, but so far, I had not met him.

Friday nights, I was with Matthew. Saturday nights with Robin and KT at my house staying up late to watch Shock Theater and eating Momma's home-made fudge.

Everybody else was moving in the fast lane, growing up, experimenting with petting, and making out in parked cars. Robin, KT, and I just wanted to have fun, laugh, cut up, act crazy, and dance to music.

I HAVE LEARNED:

"My sheep hear my voice; they know my voice, and they follow me."

(John 10:27).

#PLASTICTULIPS

11

The Voice Of God

14 years old

MOMMA AND I, with Leeann, and Charlie, had started attending a Methodist Church on the corner of Ann Street and Highland Avenue. It was a small congregation with a fiery little preacher we called Pastor Ken. A young college boy was helping Pastor Ken with the youth. He was not only good-looking and a great preacher, but he could sing.

That's when my opinion of Christian boys would change. He was in school to be a minister. I thought, "How could you look that good, and waste yourself being a preacher?" I looked forward to going to church just to see him.

One day, I was cleaning our house, and of course, the vacuum cleaner was dead, and I could not revive it. I used a broom to get the dirt out of the carpet.

The radio was blasting my favorite songs as I swept, dancing to the beat of The Beach Boys, "I Get Around."

Suddenly there was an interruption in my thoughts. I heard a voice in my head say, "You're going to be married to a preacher."

I heard the voice, but I had no control over it. The music was playing, and the voice came through my thoughts. It was like a speaker saying, "We interrupt this regularly scheduled program for a special announcement: You're going to be married to a preacher."

I stopped sweeping and stood still. I knew at that moment, God just spoke. It was like an earthquake shook in my body that makes that moment stand still in time. It was a moment that would change my life forever.

I put the broom down and went into the kitchen to call Mom. She was a bookkeeper for a women's boutique named Benson's. She answered the phone, "Mom, God just spoke to me."

There was a brief pause, and tenderly Momma asked, "What did He say?"

"Momma, I'm going to be married to a preacher."

Mom's response was with such tenderness, "Denice, that's wonderful."

Plastic Tulips in the Winter

To this day, I am still amazed at the fact that Momma didn't laugh at a fourteen-year-old telling her she just heard the voice of God.

We had never heard of anybody hearing the voice of God, except for maybe Moses in the Bible, but he saw a burning bush. Yet, Mom believed me. Back then, we didn't know the Bible said, "My sheep hear my voice; they know my voice, and they follow me" (John 10:27).

I began to think it might be that young boy from church. He was good-looking, could sing, and was a dynamic preacher. Wow, I had it all figured out for God.

####

That Friday night, Robin, KT, and I were on our way to hear a band and dance the night away. It was still early, and we didn't want to get there before the crowd, so we drove around cruising. We passed the little red brick church. I noticed the youth group standing in the front yard of the church. Bart, the handsome college boy, was there. He was helping Pastor Ken with street witnessing.

I said to Robin, and KT, "Let's stop to see what they're up to." Walking toward them, Bart shouted, "Denice, I'm glad you came to go street witnessing with us." "Oh, Bart, I'm sorry, but we already have plans to go dancing." His response was, "Denice, if you go dancing tonight, you will dance in hell."

It stopped me in my tracks, blinked my eyes to take it all in., I didn't understand. Did Bart just say that I would go to hell tonight if I went dancing instead of street witnessing? Then sternly, "You must get your priorities in order."

"Uh, wow Bart, we wanted to stop to say hello before we went dancing. I'm sorry you feel that way."

We split, putting the keys in the ignition, turned the radio up loud, perturbed at him. "I didn't know they danced in hell!" We laughed. I realized right then he didn't rock my world. I was disappointed in him. I knew right then he couldn't be the preacher God spoke about. We headed to the YMCA.

WHO'S THAT BOY

As we walked through the double doors into a big open room, the band was already rocking, and the lead singer was singing, "I Feel Good." The place was jam-packed with teenagers. Everyone had formed a circle in the room around a couple that was dancing.

"What's going on?" I asked Robin and KT as I pressed my way through the crowd to see.

Plastic Tulips in the Winter

We stood there moving to the music as we all had our eyes fixed on that couple. The boy was swift on his feet and had a confidence I had never seen. His khaki pants, and a baby-blue button-up shirt with a burgundy belt, and burgundy penny loafers, let me know he came from money. He had brown hair with sideburns that looked stylish.

My mind raced as I watched him dance with that girl. I couldn't take my eyes off him. My heart was pounding in my chest as I thought, "Where in the world did this guy come from? I could hardly breathe. What is his name?"

My eyes seemed to pierce through him as I thought, "What gives this guy the confidence I see expressed from head to toe?" He was doing the James Brown dance. I had never seen a guy dance the way he did; he was loose and tight all at the same time.

Robin elbowed me, covering her mouth so no one else could hear, "You think you can get a date with any boy, let me see you get a date with that boy." She pointed at him.

Still not willing to take my eyes off him, I responded with excitement, "Give me two weeks, and I'll have a date with him, better yet—he's the boy I'm going to marry."

Robin laughed, "Yeah, right, let's see."

The bet was on. I still believed in destiny. God's pull in my life was like a magnetic force pulling me toward Him, {God}. I didn't give any thought to how this boy would fit into the picture of what God had spoken to me.

I just knew, for the first time in my life, I felt that something bigger than life itself was right in front of me. I knew I was looking at a challenge in this guy. He looked like a man compared to every other boy. The way he handled himself shouted masculinity. His body language shouted, going places in life. He didn't wear rags. I could also tell every girl in the room would give their eyeteeth to date him. I didn't know anything about him, so with my eyes still fixed on him, I asked the girl next to me. "Who's that boy?"

She looked at me as if to say, "Where have you been?" Then, "You don't know who that is? He is a college student at the University of Alabama, and that girl he is dancing with, he's been going steady with her for the last two years."

I took my eyes off him to look at her to check out my competition. She was cute, stacked, and looked like a woman. Wearing a tight skirt with a button-up, V-neck fitted sweater, a wide belt, and a pair of flat shoes. Her highlighted blonde hair was ratted and smoothed out with bangs, styled in a flip. She wore fake eyelashes with her dark brown eyes and had big dimples on both cheeks. Her pale icy pink lipstick told me she kept up with the latest in style. I knew I looked like a little girl compared to her.

While looking at my competition, I realized the girl next to me was still talking about that boy. "He's the manager of the band that is playing, and he has his band, too. They're called 'The Swinging Jades.' He's the lead singer and plays the keyboard. She added, "His girlfriend was Miss Georgia Peach this year."

I then looked away to stare at the best-looking thing I had ever seen in my life. I thought, "You're going to need a whole lot of confidence to get in-between this guy and that girl." I leaned in closer and whispered, "What's his name?"

"Steve Vickers," she said excitedly

Right then, it felt like a flash of lightning hit me in the gut. I realized that he was the big brother of Tommy Vickers, the boy who gave me my first kiss. The same guy Janice had told me about.

The band began playing "Wooly Bully," and everybody in the room started to dance. Robin, KT, and I split up. We began dancing with the boys in the room, but my mind was on finding a way to meet that Steve Vickers.

After dancing to three other fast songs, I noticed Miss Georgia Peach had left the room. Steve was leaning against a table with his arms crossed, watching the band play. When the song ended, I turned to the boy I was dancing with, "I'm going to take a break."

I walked toward Steve, and the band began to play, "The House of the Rising Sun."

I took a deep breath, pulled my shoulders back, and told myself I had all that I needed to turn his head. I was five foot seven, slim, easy on the eyes, and not stuck up, just confident. I was wearing a short, fitted, dark purple sleeveless dress with a purple satin ribbon tied around my waist. My jet-black hair was midway down my back, and my make-up was perfect: black mascara, eyeliner, pale pink lipstick, and a pair of dangling silver loop earrings. I was going to flirt for the plain fun of it. I walked up to him and stuck out my hand to shake his, "Hi, my name is Denice Perkins," I looked straight into his eyes, and smiled.

He laughed as he reached to take my hand, and came back with a remark to make me laugh, "What do you want me to do, melt?" His eyes danced and never left mine. I have never looked into the eyes of a person that spoke to me the way his eye's did.

I thought, "What a confident jerk." Yet, it only made me more attracted to Steve. I needed a confident come back, I thought, "Quick, speak," "Hmm, Well, most boys do, why shouldn't you?" I smiled.

Leaning further back against the table, crossing his feet, and staying in total control, he smiled back with those brown eyes flashing. "I'm Steve Vickers."

"Oh, I know who you are, Steve Vickers. I just thought it was time for you to know me."

He touched me with his eyes. He started at my feet, and worked his way up, then looked me directly in the eyes, raised one eyebrow, and smiled. I felt I could melt right there, and then, but I remained calm.

Right at that moment, his girlfriend walked up. She moved in front of me and stood between us. I stepped to the side of her. She placed her hands on his shoulders and began to shake him. "Steve Vickers, I can't trust you for a moment." She looked at me as if to say, and when are you leaving?

As I spoke up, he turned his face away from her and toward me. I spoke, "I guess I better go before I cause you more trouble." I smiled.

He smiled and gave me a wink and replied, "I'll see you around."

I looked back over my shoulder to see if he was watching Miss Georgia Peach or me. His eyes were on me as I walked away.

12

Destiny

THE NEXT WEEK, destiny would come into play. Momma let me take her car so we could go to Treasure Isle, a hamburger joint. I parked the car and told Robin and KT that I would go in and get us drinks. When I walked out with a tray of cokes in my hands, I noticed the car was gone. Robin and KT had driven away to cruise up and down the Atlanta Highway. As I was looking everywhere for my car, someone suddenly tapped me on the shoulder. I turned around, and it was Mister Wonderful himself.

My heart began to race, bouncing off the walls with excitement as my face felt flushed, just looking at him. "Hey, Denice, who are you here with?" He remembered my name.

"I'm with my girlfriends, but they seem to have left me."

"Well, why don't you come sit in my car, and we'll talk while you wait for them?"

Of course, I wanted to. I had a bet with Robin that I would have a date with him within two weeks; this was my chance. I had not been able to get him off my mind. He opened his car door on the driver's side, and I slid in. I can't say I wasn't nervous.

The excitement I was feeling was equal to what I felt the first time I saw the Beatles on The Ed Sullivan Show. I wanted to scream with excitement, but I kept calm.

"So, what are your plans tonight?" He asked.

"Uhm, I don't have any, I'm just hanging out with my girlfriends."

Robin and KT pulled in about two cars away and saw me in the car with Steve.

I turned to Steve, "They're back, and I guess I'd better go." He smiled as he asked, "Why don't you tell them to come back in an hour so you and I can go for a ride? We can get to know each other."

I tilted my head to one side as I thought about my decision, "Uh...Okay, just a moment, let me go tell the girls." I was dead serious about winning the bet.

Plastic Tulips in the Winter

As I walked over to the car, I tried to keep my cool. I could see that they were ecstatic and bouncing up and down in their seats. Robin asked, "How did you do that?"

I told them how it happened, "Look, I'm going for a ride with Steve, come back, and pick me up in an hour."

He was driving a white 1960 Cadillac convertible. It was apparent Steve was from a different background than mine. It was also evident that Steve was used to the finer things. The way he dressed and the car he drove.

We drove away with the radio playing the Rolling Stones song *"Satisfaction."* Steve sang out loud as he moved to the beat of the music while tapping the steering wheel. His dark eyes flashed with such life in them. He turned, smiled at me, and kept singing. It wasn't long until, sure enough, he turned down a back road, and headed for, the Lights.

I knew everyone would ask, "Where did you go with him?" I would have to say, "The Lights." Everybody knows that is where you go to make out.

Steve parked the car and turned the music down low. I felt the back of my seat going back slowly and tilting. My mind started racing. I thought, "You better plan your next move, or he might try to rape you. Girl, you're over your head on this one." I looked around for light or maybe a house in case I needed to run.

Shifting his body toward me with his back against his window, I quickly stretched out my arms, keeping him at a distance. I was not about to let him think this was going to be a making out date, so immediately "Uhm, well... tell me about your girlfriend."

He kinda laughed as he asked, "Why do you want me to talk about her? She's not here. Let's talk about you. Let me get to know you."

I thought, "Get to know me how? Surely, he isn't going to try anything." I was melting over him but not enough, not kick him where it hurts if I had to.

His arm was resting on the steering wheel and the other on the back of the seat. He leaned forward to kiss me. However, because I was shaking, he missed and kissed me on the end of my nose. He laughed.

"I don't think I need to be here with you right now. The timing is not good." I smiled to hide how nervous I was, or should I say, how scared I was. "I better get on back to my girlfriends."

The smile he gave me was a smile like, "You're cute." Steve raised the seat back up, cranked the car, turned the radio up loud, and began to sing as he drove to take me back.

I got out of the car, leaned my head in the window, "It was good seeing you again." I was thinking, man, he looks so good.

"Yeah, you too," he smiled as he drove away.

I wasn't sure I would ever get that chance again. I jumped in the car with Robin, and KT and said, "Oh, he is so tough."

I had won the bet, but what they didn't know was I had just gotten the scare of my life. I also knew this boy had captured my mind that night.

This boy seemed bigger than life—Steve Vickers. I couldn't get him off my mind. I soon heard he broke up with his girlfriend. I would see him around town, always with a different girl in his car; blonde, brunette, or redhead—they were all beautiful and older than me.

Well, as fate would make it happen, one night, the phone rang. "Denice, this is Steve Vickers. Do you remember who I am?" Calmly I answered, "Of course, Steve, I remember you."

"How would you like to catch a movie with me tonight?"

"Sure, I would love to, what are we going to see?"

"How about, Doctor Zhivago, I'll pick you up around seven." "Great."

I hung the phone up, screamed, and ran around the room, dancing and singing, "I got it. I got it. I can't help it. It's a good thing, and I got it!" I jumped into the shower, washed my hair, rolled it, got under the dryer, put on my make-up, and dressed to kill. By the time the doorbell finally rang. I opened the door, and there he was.

Steve opened the car door for me. We went to a drive-in theater and watched the movie. He didn't even try to kiss me. He drove me home and walked me to the door. I put my hand on the doorknob, turned, and smiled, "I had a great time."

Steve gave me that gorgeous smile of his, "I did too. We'll have to do it again."

I responded, "I would like that, good night."

Plastic Tulips in the Winter

I opened the door, went into the house, and leaned against the door for a moment, just to catch my breath. When I got in bed, the phone rang.

"What are you doing?"

"I'm already in bed, why, did you forget something'?" I was surprised he called.

"No, I just got home and kept thinking about tonight, and about you, your different. Steve laughed. So, I got in bed, and just thought I would call you, and we could talk for a while."

We talked for hours laughing at each other as we shared funny stories about friends and life. I could hear him breathing over the phone. I thought his breathing was sexy. As it got later, excited, and sleepy at the same time, "Steve, I'm so sleepy I've got to hang up."

He responded, "Me too, sleep well, by the way, I had a great time tonight."

He continued to date other girls, and I knew why—I didn't put out. However, he always called me on the spur of the moment. We went out and had fun, but there were still the other girls, the girls that gave him what he wanted. He never tried anything with me, though. He could tell I wasn't that kind of girl.

CRUISING

One Saturday afternoon, Robin and I were out cruising. We pulled into Treasure Isle, where I asked a girl if she knew where Steve Vickers lived. "Go down the Atlanta Highway until there are no more businesses, and just keep driving; it's out in the country. You will see a dirt road.

We did just as she said, and as we turned down the dirt road, to my amazement, there sat a Southern plantation home. There were Pecan trees, magnolia trees, and azalea bushes with honeysuckle growing all along a fence mixed with pink baby roses.

The large white columns across the front porch were impressive. The side entrance had a porte-cochere supported by massive white columns on each side. In the back of the plantation home was a water well-built of stone with a little rounded door. It looked like the plantation home, Tara, from the movie, "Gone with the Wind." I screamed out loud, "Wow, look at that!"

Steve was on the side of the house, washing his car with the radio blasting. He was barefoot with shorts and a T-shirt. We pulled up beside him and got out. "Hey, Steve Vickers, what are you up to?" "Oh, just taking in this beautiful day, and washing my car. What are you girls up to today?"

He smiled as he pushed the sudsy sponge across the hood of the car. He dropped the hose and bent down to put the sponge into the soap bucket. I told him we were just cruising around town, checking out friends. He asked if we would go up to his house and get some liquid soap for his bucket from his mom. "Just ask my Mom for it. She'll send it down to me."

I was raised a girl does not call boys, and she does not go to his house. I was not sure what Mrs. Vickers would think.

We rang the doorbell, and a black woman in a white uniform came to the door. We asked to speak with Mrs. Vickers.

Mrs. Vickers came to the door. She was a beautiful, petite woman, with dark hair, and dark eyes, just like her son. Wearing a full-skirted cream color dress with colorful parakeets all over it, and a belt that synched in her waste. She wore beautiful gold earrings, and bracelets, and a pearl necklace.

On both hands, were the most beautiful diamond rings I had ever seen. I wondered, "Does she dress like this every day just to be around the house." She invited us in to sit down and have a Coke with her. Robin and I sat on the Victorian chairs, looking at each other while she went into the kitchen to get the drinks.

I whispered to Robin, "Look at that crystal chandelier." Robin looked as though she was going to pass out. I whispered, "Just breathe."

Mrs. Vickers returned from the kitchen with two glass bottles of ice-cold Coca -Colas with a napkin wrapped around each one. We sat for a few moments and talked to her. She was sweeter than apple pie.

Luckily, Robin didn't pass out, and we gave Steve the soap and left. As we drove away, I thought, "I swear, that boy Steve Vickers takes my breath away. If I were ever going to be a loose girl, he'd be the one I'd wanna be loose with!

Even as I said that I knew that was just not me. My innocence and understanding about my self-worth made me different. I believed there was more to me than a pretty face and a body to give away. It wasn't long after that when he called. "Are you going to hear the band tonight?"

Plastic Tulips in the Winter

I thought he was asking me so that we could be together there. I answered, "Yes. Robin, KT, and I plan on going. I'll see you there."

I was excited he was going to meet me there. "Great," was his response.

We did small talk, and then I got ready to go. When we arrived, Steve acted as if I wasn't there. He was talking to other girls, so I went into the girl's restroom to freshen up my lipstick. A girl named Jackie walked in behind me, lit up a cigarette, and leaned up against the wall across from the vanity I was using. I looked at her in the mirror as she asked, "You're Denice Perkins, aren't you?"

She took a drag off her cigarette, blew the smoke out slowly, and looked at me from behind. I glanced at her through the mirror as I rolled lipstick across my lips. She was one of the girls I had seen around him.

Acting calm, I responded, "Yes," and continued to look at her through the mirror as I combed my hair.

She took another drag off her cigarette and asked, "Would you like to know what Steve Vickers said about you?" My thought was, "Ok, I can play this game with you."

Still looking in the mirror, I responded, "Sure, what did he say?"

"He said you're a cute little girl, but he knew he could get a date with you any time he wanted to. He said it makes you not interesting." I turned to look at her as I put my brush back into my purse. "He did, did he? Well, Steve Vickers doesn't know me very well." I walked out.

Can you believe that, me not interesting? She passed me as I was walking back on to the dance floor, and she was shaking her hips as if they had purpose. Isn't that funny. Oh, I don't mean it's funny about her hips having purpose, but it's funny because I said it that way.

Well, I knew right then things were bound to change once I turn the tables on him. The girls I saw him with were older than me, and not that innocent. It was apparent he liked spending his time with them. They were usually all over him. I walked into the crowded dance room and saw Steve standing in front of the band listening to them play while some girl had her arm around his waist.

Well, of course, I was so ticked off. I was thinking," Steve thinks the sun comes up just to hear him crow." I was not only mad at him but also at myself for allowing him to see through me. He saw how excited I was to see or talk to him. I had let down my wall.

Now, I was so ready to let him know the world didn't stop when he was born. He wasn't God's gift to all women. I grit my teeth, and marched up to him, grabbed him by the arm, yanking him away from that girl, "You go to hell, Steve Vickers!"

He knew that was totally out of character and could tell I was ticked off. He didn't know what had happened, and I didn't care to explain it to him. I walked away, not giving him a chance to respond. I went straight home.

As I walked into my bedroom, I grabbed my science notebook from the shelf and wrote across the front of it with black ink*: I Denice Perkins, will not date Steve Vickers again until I am ready.* I tossed it in my closet and looked away as I threw myself across the bed and cried. I didn't like that feeling of being vulnerable. I was a Fatherless child.

I was crazy about him.

I HAVE LEARNED:

"Life is like riding a bicycle, if you fall down, you get back up."
AND
"You get backup wiser and stronger, by choice."

#PlasticTulips

13

The Challenge

HOMEWORK WAS not my cup of tea. When it came to reading science or history books, well, I guess it would've been like trying to pull my teeth. Discounting my grades, which were just passing grades life, was mostly fun at this age. But now that I'm writing my memoir, I realize it's a struggle for me. I mix verbs tenses, use commas wrong, and I can't spell! So, if you are reading this, thank you for not critiquing me.

My routine was I did my housework first, then lay across my twin bed with my pink princess phone. Just in case a friend called while I did my homework. Of course, the radio was on, Sonny and Cher were singing, "I Got You, Babe."

The phone rang. I was sure it was probably Robin wanting to know what our plans were for that night. "Hello"

"Denice, this is Steve Vickers." My heart began to race. "I thought you, and I might go out tonight."

"Oh, thanks for asking Steve, but I Uhm, have other plans." We made small talk for a few minutes and then hung up.

He called every week. It was hard saying no, and I could tell it was getting Steve. He was patient with me but persistent. He wasn't used to the answer "no" or "I have other plans" from any girl. I thought he would give up, but he continued calling.

One night he called, and he was ready for me. "Denice, do you want to go out tonight?"

"Uhm, no, Steve, I have other plans, but thanks for asking." There was a moment of silence. He spoke soft but direct. "Okay, Denice, I get it. What about we go out tomorrow night?"

He was not enjoying the chase. Steve was used to calling all the shots. I wanted more from him, and I was not going to be just another girl to him.

"Okay, Denice, what about next Friday night?"

I took in a deep breath and let it out slowly, knowing he was getting the message, and if I pushed him too far, he might give up. Again, I replied, "I have plans next Friday, too."

Plastic Tulips in the Winter

I could hear him breathing over the phone as if he had enough. "Denice, two Friday nights from now, are you right now going to tell me you already have plans?"

Soft, but firmly, I answered, "Steve, I told you, I have other plans." I continued to give him the cold shoulder in my words.

"Denice, it looks like you have plans with everybody but me." I could hear the hurt, the rejection in his voice, and his words.

I responded, "Well, Steve Vickers, it looks like you've finally got it."

I knew I was acting like a jerk. I felt terrible but also thought Steve needed it. Now, he was finally getting the message. With my mind made up, this boy was going to earn me. I was determined to stick to what I had written across my science notebook:

I, Denice Perkins, will not date Steve Vickers until I'm ready.

That night, I planned to stay home and watch TV with Momma, Leeann, and Charlie. I was already in my PJs when the doorbell suddenly rang.

As I opened the door, there he stood with both hands in his pockets. Smiling as he looked at me, "So, where are you going in your pajamas?". It was funny, oh, I don't mean that I would lie to him, but funny, I was caught red-handed.

"Uh, actually, I'm watching TV with my family tonight. That's my plan." I smiled.

"So, are you going to invite me in to watch TV with the family?"

Can you believe that! I couldn't believe it. Steve was chasing me, but I knew I had to play hardball, "No, I think you need to go out with your buddies tonight."

Throwing his hands up in the air with a gesture, "I give up, Okay," he left, shaking his head as he went. I shut the door, walked over to the window, and watched him drive away. It didn't feel right being rude. He stopped calling, and summer past. I figured I had blown it for good.

FOOTBALL

The school year always started at the end of August. It was my first year in high school, and I was now a tenth grader at Robert E. Lee High School.

The Universities of Alabama and Auburn are two Alabama colleges that divide the people of the state during football season. In the South, football is like a religion, and Saturday is its holy day. If you couldn't afford season tickets, there was no need to miss the game; people just parked their cars in the stadium parking lot, pulled out their lawn chairs, and charcoal grills, turned their transistor radios up loud, and they were there. That would become a phenomenon—tailgating.

Robert E. Lee High School, known as the Generals, and Sidney Lanier High School, named the "Poets," had the same football rivalry every year. They were the only two white public high schools in the city.

Thursday, the night before the Lee and Lanier football game, students of both schools went out to cruise the main drags. For the Lee students, Atlanta highway was the main drag with and Treasure Isle hamburger joint, Fairview Avenue with Suzy's hamburger joint was the strip for Lanier students. This night every year, they invaded each other's territory. Lanier students arrived in a procession, lining their cars up, and down the Atlanta highway on the side of the street opposite Treasure Isle. Robert E. Lee's students were ready for them as students parked their cars up and down the road.

They were standing beside their vehicles, while some sat on the hoods. Convertible tops were down and packed with students as they chanted at each other.

They trash-talk to each other about the upcoming game and debated over what the score would be for that year.

Later that night, Lee Generals, in turn, invaded Lanier Poet's territory in the same manner.

The police were everywhere, not to stop us, just to control traffic and to protect the General Lee statue from vandalism. Lanier students always found a way to paint a yellow stripe down the General's back. Lee, in turn, would find a way to distract the police during the night, and graffiti painted on the front of the building. In bright red letters, they would paint the words Robert E. Lee, and the previous year's winning score to remind them of their loss.

Steve Vickers transferred from the University of Alabama to a small college in town. He had been partying too much at his fraternity, and his grades had dropped. His parents made him come home until he brought his GPA back up. That meant I would be seeing him around town more often during the week. Every time I saw him, he was with a different girl.

I still dated Mathew on and off. One night, we were at the Lee Generals football game together. As the band played, the crowd clapped and cheered the football team onto the field as the cheerleaders ran to cheer them on.

Plastic Tulips in the Winter

I scanned the bleachers behind me, and Steve was high up in the bleachers with his friends. I turned, "Matthew, I'm going to the restroom. I'll be right back."

He asked, "Do you want me to go with you?"

"No," I answered quickly. "You just watch the game. I'll be right back."

I walked up the bleachers to get to the landing that entered the concession stand. Steve saw me, just as I'd hoped. When I walked out of the restroom, Steve was waiting for me. "Oh, hey, Steve." I smiled and continued walking.

"You look nice tonight," as he flashed that gorgeous smile. "Are you here with anyone?"

I was glad to answer, "I'm with Matthew Folsom."

We talked, but the conversation was mostly centered around asking me questions like, "How long have you been dating Matthew?" or "Tell me why you will date him, but you won't go out with me?"

"Because I'm not ready. I don't want to date you, Steve Vickers. Not until I'm ready."

Looking slightly confused, he asked, "Ready for what?" He had a look in his eyes that seem to shoot right through me. I answered, "You, Steve Vickers, ready for you."

I could tell it rattled his cage. He just didn't get it; I wanted more than he was willing to give.

He asked, "Are y'all going anywhere after the game?" "I'm not sure why?"

Waiting to see what he was going to say. "Why don't you get him to take you home early, and I'll call you?" My heart told me, why not, just talk on the phone with him. I stopped walking and turned to face him. Looking into his dark brown eyes, I moved in closer, touched his arm, "Okay, sure. Give me a call."

I realized that night on the phone. Steve had never had a conversation like this with a girl. We talked about life and what we both wanted.

Steve knew Matthew; they had a few classes together at school. He began to speak to Matthew, giving him dating advice. It was his way of trying to stay in my business.

####

That next week, I was walking home from school and noticed Steve's car parked out in front of my house. Can you believe that? He was just leaning against the car, acting like he was doing something important. His were feet crossed, smoking a cigarette, listening to his radio.

Walking toward him, I playfully shouted, "What are you doing in front of my house, Steve Vickers?" Thinking, how cool is this that he just dropped by?

"I've got something I want to ask you." As he took one more drag from his cigarette, threw it on the ground, and pressed it out with his shoe.

Holding my books, I relaxed my posture and leaned against his car next to him. "So, what's up? Let me have it. What is this big question, Steve Vickers?" I giggled.

Looking him in the eyes, as I was thinking, "He doesn't realize how much he makes me melt."

He spoke, "Matthew's is going to ask you to go steady with him. What's your answer going to be?"

"Not that it's any of your business Steve Vickers, but my answer will be no."

"Denice, if I ask you to go steady with me, not to date anyone but me, would you?"

"Oh, Steve Vickers, flattery will get you nowhere with me." I giggled, "Besides, I'm not going steady with anybody. I don't want to be committed to any one guy. I want to be free to date who I want when I want.

So, Steve Vickers, if you're asking if I could be off the market, the answer is no." I smiled, just loving this moment. I knew the ball was now in my court.

Steve had this expression—his left eyebrow would rise when he was uncomfortable about something. I told him I had to go on into the house to get the dishes washed before Mom got home. He drove away, and as he did, I thought about how different our two lives were. He went home to housekeepers and a cook. He had it made in the shade.

14

I Want It All

EVERY YEAR IN October, the fair came. We heard Steve's band was going to be playing at the fair this year, and so I was sure I would see him.

I wore black and white herringbone hip-hugger pants with a white leather belt. The top was a sleeveless, black, fitted, V-neck shirt laced with a white shoestring on the front with just the right amount of skin showing on my waste.

Walking through the crowd on the Fair Ground, I saw Steve and his bandmates from a distance walking toward me. I pretended not to see him. I was laughing and busy talking to Robin as we passed. He turned, came up behind me, and grabbed me by the arm, swinging me around to face him. "Do you know what you look like?"

I just stared at him, waiting to hear what he was going to say. His eyes flashed with anger. He continued, "Denice Perkins, you look like a French whore, and the girl I'm going to marry is not going to look like this!"

Jerking my arm away from him and not knowing what a French whore was, but it sounded nasty, so I said," and what makes you think I'm going to marry you?"

He talked back as if he were my boss. "You are going to go out with me tomorrow night, and you're not giving me any excuses."

He waited for my reply, expecting me to say no. I was stunned at his boldness. I thought about it for a moment, and then, with an upbeat attitude, "Okay, tomorrow night, see you then." I felt like I was ready, and that this time... he was ready for me.

The next night, as I got in his car, there was a bottle of champagne that I had to push out of the way so that I could slide over. "Here, hold these," handing me two champagne glasses.

We hadn't even gone a block before I spoke up, "Take me home." He pulled the car over. "What's wrong?"

"I'm not going out with you if you're going to drink." Frustrated, he threw the glasses out the window. "Steve, if you're going to date me, there will be no cussing, no drinking, and you will be in church with me Sunday morning."

Looking at me, he moaned, "What, you have got to be kidding me."

The determined look on my face told him I was not kidding. From that night on, we went out together, and Steve was in church with me on Sunday. Only one time, he called, "I'm not going to make it to church today."

I answered him with, "Well, that's something. I'm not going to be available for our next date." Steve made it to church that day. I saw him sitting on the last pew as I was walking out.

FILL MY CUP LORD

One Sunday night at church, Bart, the guy who told me I was going to dance in hell, was singing a solo, *"Fill My Cup Lord."* I cried as he sang.

After church, Steve and I went back to my house and sat on the swing in the backyard. He asked, "Denice, why were you crying tonight when that boy was singing?

I didn't tell him. I was thinking about the day I was sweeping the carpet and heard God Speak. I knew Steve was far from being a preacher, but I also knew I was falling in love with him.

After a few minutes of silence, looking up at the stars, and knowing God had to be bigger than I understood, "Steve, I just want all God has for me. I don't want to miss my destiny in Him."

It shook Steve to his core. His shoulders hunched, and he gazed to the ground. 'He had never met a girl that took life this seriously.

"Denice, you need to go get you one of those church boys. You don't need to be around me. I hurt people. I want to be a good person, but I guess some people are just born bad. I ruin everything I touch. You need to run from me. Don't get me wrong, I want you so bad that it hurts, but you're different—more so than any other girl I've ever met. I can't help but admire you, Denice, and I'm telling you, you need to run."

I knew right then; I was not going to run. It was too late. I was in love with him.

By this point, Steve had already told me that he loved me several times, but I couldn't say it back to him. To me, the word love meant pain. He'd ask me to tell him I loved him, but I just couldn't. I'd say to him, "Love hurts. It hurts to say; I love you. Steve, how many girls have you said that to just to get what you want from them? There is too much pain in love."

He looked at me, "Yes Denice, but I mean it when I say it to you. I now know that I have never truly been in love. Denice, I am in love with you."

The sincerity in his voice made me throw my arms around him. "Steve Vickers, someday I'm going to marry you, and have a little boy named Stephen. He is going to look just like you." He smiled at me saying, "You are, huh?"

I pushed his hair back away from his eyes, "Yes, I am. You're my man one day Steve Vickers..."

WHAT HAVE YOU DONE?

As the months passed, our friends were still getting drafted off to war. One afternoon as I was standing at the sink washing dishes, Steve's car pulled up in front of the house. I walked out to greet him, as he stepped out of the car, I was shocked to see him wearing a sailor's uniform with his head shaved. My heart was in my mouth, "Steve, what have you done?"

"Denice, my number was coming up, and I would get drafted off to Nam. If I were going to war, I would rather be on a ship, so I joined the Navy. I will have to serve six years, and three of them in full-time duty.

Denice, I'm going away for those three years. Will you wait for me?"

I looked at him, "What, No, I won't wait. I can't just throw my youth away waiting for a boy who will be gone for three years and hope he doesn't forget me."

He responded, "Then, let's get married."

A few nights later, we were on a date. Steve parked the car; the rain was pattering down onto the ground and sliding down the window.

He was sweating, but he didn't care; this was his moment. He reached over to the glove compartment and pulled out a little white velvet box, and he rapidly changed his position in his seat toward me. "Denice, I love you. I love you more than life itself. I need you in my life, and I will not lose you because of this war. I need to know right now: do you love me? Can you love me for the rest of your life?" I responded, "Yes."

"Denice, Will you marry me?"

Knowing he was all I wanted, "Yes, Steve, I do love you, and I will marry you." I was sixteen, and Steve was twenty. The wedding date set for August 4, 1967.

June rolled around. I had already seen a doctor and started birth control. By this point, Steve and I were into heavy kissing.

Plastic Tulips in the Winter

One night we were parking, lying down in the seat, making out in each other's arms. I didn't want to wait any longer. I wanted Steve to touch me and make love to me. "If you want me, Steve, you can have me."

Everything about him changed at that moment. He sat up, cranked the car, and took me home. Before I got out of the car, he looked at me and said, "I want you so badly. Believe me, when I say, I want you. I always thought if given a chance, I would take you, but I can't hurt you like that. I'll wait for you."

I went into the house, washed my make-up off, and got into the bed. I lay there in my thoughts; I had offered myself to Steve, and he had turned me down. He loved me. He cared about my true feelings, and not those made in an emotional moment. I could not wait until the day we'd be intimate.

Once again, a few nights later, we found ourselves in the same state of passion, but this time, we didn't stop. I offered myself to Steve. Afterward, without saying a word, Steve started the car, and we drove away. I stared out the window as we rode in silence. Steve turned the car into the parking lot of the Methodist Church his mother attended.

It was a beautiful stone church with massive Gothic doors with iron hinges. It was late at night, and the building was dark. He got out of the car, walked over to the passenger side, and opened the car door. Steve grabbed me by the hand and walked me up to the front stairs of the church. He put his hand on the big heavy door handle, and it was not locked. The stained-glass windows lit up as the streetlights shone through them. The church had high ceilings and massive wooden beams. He sat me down on the front pew, knelt in front of me, and grabbed my hands. He wept, "Denice, I am so sorry."

I couldn't stop crying. "Steve, it was my choice too.

15

Marriage, And Suspicions

THE NEXT FEW weeks I was busy planning the wedding. Robin was my maid of honor, Leeann, my flower girl, and Charlie, my baby brother, a handsome little boy with green eyes, and blonde curls, my ring bearer. Pam and Janice were bridesmaids, along with my girlfriends. They all wore fuchsia satin empire waist, bell-shaped full-length gowns. After saying our vows, the minister turned us toward the congregation as he spoke, "Ladies and gentlemen, I would like to introduce to you, Mr. and Mrs. Steve Vickers."

The organ played as we walked down the aisle and exited the auditorium into the foyer of the church. Steve grabbed me and spun me around in a circle saying, "We did it. You are mine.

Plastic Tulips in the Winter

After driving for about an hour, arriving at our honeymoon suite, Steve opened the door and swept me up in his arms. We both began to laugh as he swung me around in his arms. We kissed, and he told me, "Denice Vickers, I love you." As he put me down, "Go into the bathroom, change, and I will open this bottle of champagne." I felt it was okay for that particular night.

I changed into my sheer, white, baby-doll pajamas with tiny pink roses across the top and wondered if I should leave my bra on. I was nervous. I knew I was going to have to let him see me naked eventually, so I took the bra off.

I cracked the door to see Steve putting the champagne bottle on ice. He was wearing pajama bottoms and no shirt.

How do I make my entrance? Without further hesitation, I threw open the door, jumped to the center of the bed, grabbed the pillow, and covered myself. Everything worked out the way honeymoons always do.

We came home to a little red brick house we had rented on Atlanta Highway. Mrs. Vickers bought us all new furniture and appliances. I had never had new things.

It looked like our marriage was off to a good start. Nevertheless, my insecurities about men and Steve's ways were soon to be roadblocks in my quest for happiness.

CHIPMUNK BRENDA

Steve attended his reserve meetings. He took a job in the camera department of a store. He was around beautiful women all day, that bothered me. It wasn't long before he received orders to go to the Great Lakes Naval Training Station in Illinois. I was going with him. We packed our U-Haul truck and decided to stay the night at the Vickers house.

There was an office party at a girl's house that night. I didn't want to go, but Steve said the party was for him. Everyone was drinking and dancing with everybody else's spouse. Steve was dancing with all the women. He reminded me of Daddy.

Then there was Brenda, who looked and acted loose. Her breasts pushed up and out, overflowing in her bra. Her fried, bleached blonde hair rested against her brown tan but failed to cover the sun damage on her face. She looked like a dried-up prune with fake eyelashes and shiny pink lipstick. She wore a tank top and hot pants. I do know that trashy doesn't have to have a pretty face to turn heads.

Brenda walked over, "Denice, you're so cute," in a cutie patootie way.

Plastic Tulips in the Winter

I responded, "Thank you," thinking, nature had played a cruel trick on her.

Two other girls joined in the conversation and were in appearance, just as trashy. The three of them stood in front of me and had me backed up against the wall. One asked as she took a sip from her Budweiser and holding a cigarette in the other, "So, baby, how long have you, and Steve been married?"

The three of them giggled. The thing I knew about myself was that I was only helpless when my nail polish was wet. Even then, I could pull a trigger. I answered them, knowing I was their entertainment.

"We've been married for a year."

I looked down as I was looking for a way to get away from the fort, they built around me.

I thought they had fallen out of an ugly tree and hit every branch on their way down. I'm visual.

You may be thinking right now, that I shouldn't have such a mean, judgmental attitude toward them. But haven't you ever heard, when you feel a little intimidated, you picture that person naked. Well, there you go. Now you get my drift, attempting to hold myself up when you feel forces are trying to pull you down.

Brenda then asked, "Have you gotten the itch to flirt with other men yet, Denice?" They laughed, elbowing each other, holding their beer.

The thing about a Southern girl is she will act helpless and confused when it's to her advantage. She never lets them know how clever and capable she really is.

I answered her, "Hmm, No, I don't plan on getting an itch," they thought that was funny too.

Can you believe that, an ITCH!

Brenda looked at me, "Well, honey, you will, trust me. Life can get a little boring if you don't dabble a little on the side. Your still young but the itch will come."

One of the girls tapped her on the shoulder, "Brenda, you leave her alone, don't put your ways into her; she's sweet." They giggled.

I thought, "Sweet? Did she say, Sweet? I may look sweet, but in my mind, I was talking to three chipmunks."

Walking between them to release myself, I looked back, their way again. Brenda was checking Steve out as if she had a secret with him. I walked over to Steve and asked, "Why is she looking at you that way?"

Plastic Tulips in the Winter

Sheepishly, he answered, "Oh, she's the store tramp. Don't pay her any mind." I told him I was ready to leave, so we left the party.

The next morning, I was still bothered by the night before, so I decided to look in Steve's wallet. There it was—a slip of paper with a phone number penciled on it. I wondered whose it was. I kept telling myself, no big deal, but I had to know.

I dialed the number and asked, "Who's speaking, please?" "Brenda," was her response.

It was her, the tramp, Chipmunk Brenda. She was making a play for my husband. I slammed the phone down and went to Steve to show him the piece of paper. That was my green thread.

"What is this, Steve?" I held it up in front of his face. It was my green thread coming back to haunt me. "What are you doing? Why would you take her phone number? By taking her number, you made her feel you were interested," I felt my blood boiling.

"Well, she was just trying to let me know if I have time, come see her before I leave town—as a friend."

I looked at Steve as I turned to leave the room. "Yeah, right. Are you that stupid to think I would believe that? Steve, don't you even get it."

Denice Vickers

My heart was pounding, and my face was flush. I screamed, "Steve, I am not going to do this dance with you." I looked at him feeling helpless, "Steve, don't you know, all I ever want is you."

He just looked at me with a deep stare. I knew he only wanted me, but he just couldn't be faithful. He was going to hurt me, and I wasn't emotionally ready. As a fatherless child, I knew the rug was going to be jerked from under my feet. So, I made a choice to fight my way. It was the only way I knew.

I went straight into the other room to call the chipmunk.

"Hello, Brenda, this is Denice Vickers, you know, Steve Vickers' wife.

"Oh, hello, Sunshine." I wanted to say, Hello, Chipmunk, but I held my composure.

I continued, "Steve gave me the lowdown on you. He gave me your phone number. He was laughing about how you tried to make a play for him. Do you want to know what my husband said about you, Brenda? He told me you're the store tramp, and you try to go with younger men. He was saying the men at work say you've been beaten with an ugly stick. Is that true, Brenda? He said it's the only way you can make yourself feel young again. Are you still trying to step into the past? Has life chewed you up, and spit you out, honey?"

She started huffing and puffing, but I kept talking. "Oh Brenda, let me help you on this honey, stay out of the sun. It's not working to your advantage. Oh, and I have one last important question to ask you while I have you on the phone. What are you going to do for a face when the monkey wants his butt back?"

She responded in anger, "What did you just say to me?"

"Sorry, Brenda, it's too late for you. It's my time now. You need to be young and fresh like me. You've been chewed up and spit out."

I slammed the phone down, got in the car, and went to speak with Pastor Ken. I was going to tell him about the phone number and ask him if I should go with Steve to Illinois. The pastor wasn't home, so I sat in the car, and did some self-talking to calm down, to think straight.

My heart said one thing, and my mind said another. "You don't know anything for sure. Steve just took her number; he didn't go see her. You love him. You can start over." The very next morning, we loaded the truck and left.

You may be wondering why I didn't leave him. Why did I get in that truck? My heart was in pain. Pain doesn't listen to reason, but I chose to go. Gaining experience wasn't always peaceful, especially during my early years of anxiety.

Now, it is important to me that you understand the pain, torment, jealousy, and insecurity were all there. I felt fragile, but there is still freedom of choice, and our choices determine our future. I wondered, where is God? I always had this sense that he was watching me, but I needed Him to Interrupt my life. Get involved.

16

God, Where Are You?

WE MOVED TO GREAT LAKES, Illinois. Steve was in training, and they would assign him to a ship. He and I loved each other, but we were two people going in two different directions. He had something wild and sneaky about him. Lies rolled off his tongue with ease. I was always catching him in lies. I thought, "God, have I blown my life, my destiny you had planned for me? Help me, God. Help me." I knew I was my mother's daughter.

I read books on how to find happiness, success, how to be a total woman, and whatever self-help books were out there. Buying six books at a time and read them on my lunch break.

I went to church by myself because Steve just wouldn't get out of bed. After the service, the pastor stood in the doorway, shaking everyone's hands. I walked by, and he grabbed my hand, "We are glad you visited with us this morning."

I looked at the pastor and began to cry. "Please help me. pastor, please help me."

I was searching for just one person who would stand up and say, "I have the answer. Here is what you've got to do."

I cried out, but the pastor didn't know what to do. I heard his voice echo in my soul. He patted me on the back, pushed me through the crowd, and out the door. "Now, you come back and visit us, you hear?"

I sat in the parking lot and beat the steering wheel as I screamed. "God, where are you? God, what about me? What about me? Do you even care? Do you have any answers for me? I don't care what you have done in everybody else's life. You have got to do something in my life. I'm so tired of searching for you, and never find you. God, if you are here, you must be bigger than this. I am so tired; I need your help. Are you so small you can't prove yourself to me?"

I had this pull to find out who God is. Did he put us down here to survive all the hurt and pain life dishes out? We live for ourselves, hurting each other, and then we get to go to heaven? Is that how small God is? Is that the all-powerful God?

Plastic Tulips in the Winter

On the other hand, can God possibly be so significant in this thing we call life, that He could step into our life, and truly make a difference? Can He turn things around? Is it possible, God can move on my behalf?

I dried my eyes, cranked the car, and drove home to Steve. He was watching football and had no clue about what was going on inside me.

I've always felt God had big plans for me. It's hard to explain. I am one of those people that believes there is a treasure out there, and God is going to lead me to it. I felt, if something great is going to happen, it's going to happen to me. I just had a strong sense of destiny all my life.

PAM'S WORD FOR THE DAY

The ship Steve would be on was in port in Norfolk, Virginia, for two months. The great thing was, Pam and her husband were there. His ship was out to sea. Pam and her baby girl Melissa, a toddler, were living alone. Pam told me to come and stay with her for those two months. That way, Steve could come home to me every night.

She was so excited when I arrived, and of course, looked beautiful as always. She had a cute figure, and her hair was in the same short blonde hairstyle with bangs. She showed me her little apartment and asked me how Janice, Momma, Charlie, and Leeann were doing.

I caught her up on all the latest news. Janice had gotten a divorce, again and called to say she met a truck driver, and that he invited her to go on the road for a few days with him to a music concert that's going to last three days. She told me to tell Mom not to worry about her, and to keep the boys for her until she got back.

She seemed flighty, but we didn't know at the time she was Bipolar. The event was outside of the town of Woodstock. It became known as a moment that changed the history of Rock and Roll. Janice always seemed to have that wild hair Pam, and I didn't have. Pam and I talked about it and just laughed together about Janice's hippie style of dressing.

Pam was always trying to advise me. We were outside, hanging damp clothes on the clothesline together while listening to a transistor radio. Pam said, "Let me tell you what I am doing. I keep a Webster's Dictionary beside my toilet. Every day I learn a new word and its definition."

Plastic Tulips in the Winter

She snapped a clothespin to the damp clothes on the line. She continued, "While you are here, I want you to start doing this."

I replied, "Why would I want to do that?" I had no desire to use words that I couldn't understand." I responded, "Why would I want to put people through that when I speak?" If I had to look up a word, I just wouldn't use it.

She laughed at me, "Denice so that you will become polished."

I interrupted, "But I don't want to be polished. I am as smooth as I want to be."

She stopped pinning clothes on the line, put her hands on her waist, and in a firm, correcting way, "Denice it will make you a great speaker."

"Pam, I don't want to be a great speaker. I like who I am."

She continued hanging the damp clothes on the line, ignoring my answer, and instructing me on how to become polished. "Denice, here is what you will do, take your new word for the day, and use it in a sentence."

"Pam, you go ahead and get polished. I'm as smooth as I wanna be." I showed her my dance moves.

"Okay, Pam, here is my new word for the day, Cracked." She looked at me, knowing I was goofing off and instructed me to use it in a sentence.

I answered, "Blessed is Pam, who is cracked in the head, for it is she who lets the light in."

She laughed, "Okay, get on with yourself, be who you are, Denice." We laughed and enjoyed every minute of our time together, even though it was short.

JANICE JOPLIN

The USS Albany, Steve's ship, went to St Thomas in the Virgin Islands for a couple of months. I moved to Jacksonville, Florida, to be near the port when his ship returned to the states. I was busy at work. I was a bank teller, which helped pass the time until he was back. We had already met some other sailors and their wives who lived in an apartment building near ours.

The ship returned to port, and one of the sailors and his wife had a welcome home party. Two single sailors that were on Steve's ship had a bunch of photos they had taken on the beach in St. Thomas.

Steve would not let them show me the photos. One of the guys spoke up, "He just doesn't want Denice to see what he and Janice Joplin were doing on the beach."

Plastic Tulips in the Winter

The other sailor cut his eyes at him as if to say, "Shut your mouth."

Janice Joplin was an American singer-songwriter known for her blues, and rock music. She was an icon for her counterculture movement in the USA and had performed the night before in St. Thomas. Now I hear he spent the day on the beach with her. She was known for her wild lifestyle and heavy drug use.

Steve shoved his hands in his pockets, knowing I was going to question him. "Steve, what was on those photos?"

Stammering as he spoke, and looking down at the ground, he answered, "Nothing. Janice Joplin was there on the beach that day. That's all it was."

I started to feel sick to my stomach with what I feared to be true. "No, those guys said you were sunbathing with her. How did you end up with her, and what did you do with her?" I knew that girls sunbathed nude on those beaches.

He wouldn't look me in the eyes. "Nothing, just hanging out on the beach."

My heart and mind raced as I kept pushing for information. "Then why did you grab the photos from them as they were about to show me?"

That same guy spoke up as if he wanted Steve to be exposed, "Steve was putting lotion on her." He said quickly.

I felt myself shaking inside. I never saw the photos, and Steve would not give me any straight answers. In my heart, I thought he had sex with her.

He said he didn't want to talk to me anymore about it and to stop asking questions.

Taking on my mother's pattern of playing detective, I tried to find a clue to prove Steve was unfaithful. I looked in his pockets for the telltale green thread. I examined his collars for signs of make-up, continually imagining that Steve was out with another girl when he was supposed to be on the ship. I just didn't trust him. I knew I was going to be hurt by him because that is what men do. They hurt you, don't they? At least, that is the way I felt about my life.

One day I dropped Steve off to board the ship that was leaving for its nine-month tour. As I looked at him, I slightly smiled, and in a soft tone, "I missed my period, but it's too early to do a pregnancy test."

He smiled, "You mean a baby?"

Tilting my head to the side in a shy manner. "Yes, maybe."

Plastic Tulips in the Winter

I moved home to live with Momma, and a month later, I saw the doctor. "If the rabbit dies, you're pregnant." Back then, doctors would shoot a valve of your urine into the rabbit's hip, and if the rabbit died, you were pregnant. A few days later, the doctor's office called. "Denice, the rabbit died. You're pregnant."

I wrote a letter to Steve to tell him that he was going to be a daddy.

He wrote back, "I am so happy about you and me having a baby together. You are the love of my life."

I was nineteen years old and would turn twenty just after the birth of my first child. Steve was twenty-four.

MORE OF GOD

One evening, Momma and I were sitting at the kitchen table, talking over a cup of coffee. "Denice, why don't we spend these nine months you're going to be with me searching for God together? Let's not limit our search to Baptist or Methodist just because we were born and raised Baptist. Let's not limit God to a denomination. We'll begin our search this Sunday and visit a different church in the city every week."

So, we visited Evangel Temple. Mom said, "I keep hearing something is happening there." I laughed and wrinkled my nose. "What could be happening in a church?" That was enough to make us want to visit.

We entered the auditorium with Gothic arched rafters made with tie beams of timber. There were dark stained wood pews with hunter green carpet running down the aisles toward the altar. In the choir loft, there was a Baptismal in front of a stained-glass window.

We sat on the last pew just as the people started singing, clapping, and raising their hands in the air as they rejoiced in song. I whispered to mom, "Why are they raising their hands as they sing?" Momma elbowed me to be quiet.

Jokingly, "They can't possibly all have to go to the bathroom at the same time." Again, she elbowed me as she laughed. "Hush."

The pastor began to speak as he paced the platform back and forth with his fist in the air, red-faced with every vein in his neck bulging. Boy, he was preaching. I had never heard anyone preach with such passion. As he paced, everybody's head turned to follow him.

A woman stood up and gave a message in tongues. I was sure she was from a foreign country. The pastor interpreted what she had to say. The service ended, Mom and I headed toward the door. A woman walked up, hugged me, "We are so glad to have you here today, Sister."

Every night at the kitchen table, the service became the topic of our conversation. "Momma, that just isn't for me. That woman thought I was her sister." Mom laughed.

ME, EUROPE!

The USS Albany was going to be in port in Europe. Steve asked me to come. Quickly I scraped up enough money to fly to Germany. From there, I took a flight to Switzerland and headed to the train station in Geneva, where Steve and I were to meet.

All around the station were little flower shops, gift shops, and restaurants. While I was waiting for Steve's train to arrive, I decided to buy a postcard to mail to Momma. I noticed a man in a business suit watching me. No one seemed to speak English. I was trying to determine if the box on the wall was a mailbox or trashcan. The man was still following me. When I stopped walking, he stopped walking.

I saw two young men behind the counter that sold hotdogs. I thought if I stayed by them, I would be safe. Suddenly he walked up to me and began speaking in French. I thought to myself as he was talking, this man is trying to pick me up. I must let him know with my expression, if I said, "No," that I meant it.

He whispered again as he got closer. I thought he isn't going to understand what I am about to say, but he will get it by my response.

I looked at him, threw my head back, and said very firmly, "Shut up!" He raised his eyebrows and took off running.

The two boys that were selling hotdogs realized what he said to me, and I guess they understood me because they began laughing, and were hitting each other on the back, as I walked away.

I now know that French men think a woman is at her most beautiful time when she is pregnant. He probably complimented me.

Steve didn't arrive on the train that day. It was getting dark, so I decided to rent a room for the night. I took a taxi to the nearest hotel, locked the door, and pushed the chest of drawers up against the door.

I rose early the next morning and returned to the train station to look for Steve. He arrived late that night and stayed a block away from my hotel. When he saw me, we ran toward each other, but instead of grabbing me, he grabbed my belly. "Denice, you're so beautiful." Steve had not seen me pregnant. I was seven months along and showing.

We stayed in Geneva for a few days and then flew to Nice, France, on the Riviera. It was lovely- the little shops and cafes were adorable. Frank Sinatra was there on his yacht. We spent the day at Monaco hoping to catch a glimpse of Grace Kelly and Prince Rainier. Walking the streets of the Riviera together, Steve could hardly take his eyes off me. He said he wanted to capture every moment being with me. Steve seemed nervous and tense, though. I could tell being out to sea was getting to him, and he missed home.

"Denice," he began, "I can't take it any longer. I miss you. I'm going to finish this time, and not sign up for any more years of duty." Biting his lower lip, he paused, "Denice, you are what's right in my life. I just don't want to be away from you anymore."

We spent several days on the Riviera. We sat in the park discussing names for the baby. "Steve, if it's a girl, I would like to name her Stacy."

I returned to the States, knowing the next time I saw Steve would be at the Montgomery airport with our new baby in my arms.

Denice Vickers

17

Free At Last

IT WAS GETTING close to the birth of my baby. I moved in with Pam and her two children. She had moved back to Montgomery and rented an apartment around the corner from Mom. Her husband's ship was also out at sea for a while. We split the rent. Pam and her daughter slept in one bedroom, and I slept in the other bedroom in a twin bed, sharing the room with her son, who was in his baby bed.

One night, Pam came into my bedroom and touched me on my shoulder to wake me. She was crying. "Denice, wake up."

"What? What is it? What's wrong, Pam?"

Just as when we were young kids, she asked, "Can I get in bed with you? I'm afraid." I scooted over as she slipped in beside me. Here we were, two young married girls, her with two children, and me as pregnant as

179

pregnant could be, both sharing one twin bed. We spooned together, melting into one, just like when we were children.

We cuddled while I asked her, "What are you scared of?" She whispered in my ear, "I'm scared of dying. I'm scared of being placed in a coffin. I'm scared of being placed under the ground." She was smothering in fear.

I jumped up out of bed and turned on the light. In a firm but caring voice, "Pam, I am tired of this. I am tired of you dealing with this fear, and we are going to get rid of it. I want this fear to be gone, out of your life, once, and for all."

She trembled, weeping, "I don't want this torment anymore, Denice."

I walked over to the telephone, called the little fiery preacher from the Methodist church we attended before Mom, and I started looking around. It was the middle of the night; I woke him up. I told him Pam, and I needed help. "My sister needs prayer. I apologize for calling so late, but pastor, this can't be put off any longer."

I asked if he could come over, and within thirty minutes, Pam, and I were standing in our flannel pajamas talking to him. I was doing all the talking, trying to explain to Pastor Ken how long Pam had battled fear. Looking back on this, I think it's funny— we didn't even think about getting dressed. Bless that pastor's heart. But we were covered up.

I told him, "Pam is full of fear, and we are ready for her to be free. Pastor, can God take this fear away if we give it to him?" Pam cried with her face, buried in her hands as I talked.

He walked over to Pam, put his hands-on top of her head, and commanded the spirit of fear to leave her. I had never heard or seen anything like that done, but we wanted help.

Pam, weeping, repeatedly saying, "Yes, yes, leave me." We were all praying out loud and agreeing.

We thanked the pastor for coming, and he left. Pam was free at last and never dealt with fear again. It was a miracle. She slept like a baby that night in her bed.

We would learn one day in the future that the Bible says, "Whom the Son of God sets free, is free indeed" (John 8:36). The bible also says: "Fear hath torment." God knows I'm telling you the truth. Pam was set free that night, never tormented with fear again.

The next morning, I woke up thinking I had wet the bed. Pam walked into my room, and I told her, "I wet the bed."

"Denice, you're in labor! Your water broke."

Pam put her two small children in the car and called Momma, Janice, and the Vickers to tell them to meet us at the hospital. Everyone was at the hospital except Steve. His ship was at port in Athens, Greece.

I gave birth to our baby girl, Stacy Elaine Vickers. Steve received a telegraph announcing the birth.

THE WHITE BELT

One-night, Pam, Janice, Momma, and I were sitting at the kitchen table, having a cup of coffee. Pam told us when she was in the third grade, our cousin made her do things. He was a married man with children of his own. That didn't stop him from taking Pam to the swing in the back yard, expose himself, and make her do things.

Our cousin always wore a white belt. At night, she kept seeing that white belt in her sleep, and that's why Pam always wanted to sleep between Janice and me with her legs and arms intertwined. It made her feel safe from the white belt. He warned her, if she told anyone, he would put her in a coffin and bury her in the ground. Pastor Ken had prayed for her, and the fear was gone. Now Pam could talk about it.

Janice got so mad when Pam told us; she went straight and called our cousin on the phone to tell him off. It was at least thirteen years since we had seen him. Let me tell you, and it's not smart to fall into the hands of an outraged Janice.

The phone call she made that night scared the fool out of him. I think she said something about nail gunning his penis to a tree. All he could do was stutter on the other end of the phone. He never came around again. I did have the thought that if we had had a real daddy, he would have protected his daughters. However, as we had learned, we had to stand up for ourselves.

Pam and I realized that the night the pastor came over, laid his hands on her head, and told the spirit of fear to leave her, it worked.

####

Pam's daughter Melissa had seizures since birth. She would start choking on her tongue as her eyes rolled back into her head. The doctor told Pam to hold her tongue down with a spoon until the seizure was over. It scared us; it was getting worse and happening daily.

One afternoon, Pam and I was pushing our baby strollers down the street. Melissa, who was around three, began to convulse. Her eyes rolled back in her head, and she started choking on her tongue.

Pam began to panic. I picked Melissa up out of the stroller, laid my hands-on top of her head, commanded the seizures to stop. It worked. She never had a seizure again. God knows I'm telling you the truth.

My favorite scripture in the future will be Mathew 11:12, "The kingdom of Heaven suffers violence, and the violent take it by force." In other words, [If God's Word said it is mine, then it is mine to have in this life, but I must take it by force through prayer, the Word of God, and the confession of my tongue.]

I HAVE LEARNED:

If God's Word said it is mine, then it is mine to have in this life.

BUT

I must take it by force through prayer, the Word of God, and the confession of my tongue.

Prayer= Talk to God about it.

Word= Find a scripture that relates to your problem AND.........

Confess out loud to yourself and God.

THERE IS POWER IN AGREEMENT WITH GOD.

#PlasticTulips

Steve was home for three weeks.

He returned when Stacy was ten months old.

18

The Comforter

1970

STEVE WAS GIVEN a three-week leave from his ship. It was going to be his first time meeting his daughter, Stacy Elaine Vickers. I dressed her in a beautiful pink gown and wrapped her in a soft pink blanket.

As I watched people coming off the airplane, my eyes went straight to the sailor in a white uniform. There was my man that always took my breath away. Our eyes met as he ran toward me. We kissed, and he looked down at her and smiled. "She's beautiful," kissing my face as he looked at her.

Even though it was going to be a short leave home, we decided to take advantage of the opportunity and buy a home with a VA Loan. We found one in a new subdivision. It was a three-bedroom, two-bath home with around 1200 square feet.

We waited for all the paperwork with the mortgage company. It would be a month before Stacy, and I could move in. In the meantime, Steve went back to the ship, and we stayed with Momma.

She was attending Evangel Temple. I was looking forward to attending a service. We arrived late, so we sat in the back of the church in the last pew. Buell Pitts, an evangelist, walked up to the microphone. "Tonight, my sermon is on the gift of the Holy Spirit. God has a gift for you to receive."

Then, with a strong exhortation, he declared, "He is called, "The Comforter."

I had never heard of anything like that. I couldn't understand what the pastor meant by the gift of the Holy Spirit. My mind began to race with thoughts of the mess my life was in, knowing that one day Steve and I would get a divorce and wondering what Steve was up to as the ship pulled into all those ports in the Mediterranean. I had a hard time focusing on the sermon. He sang out his sermon as the congregation backed him.

"This gift will give you Joy."

"Amen, brother," the people shouted.

"This gift will give you Peace."

Plastic Tulips in the Winter

"That's right, Sir." A lady spoke up as she agreed.

"This gift will give you Assurance."

"Yes, it will." Another shouted out from the congregation.

He threw his hand up in the air, held his Bible up, and declared, "The Holy Spirit brings comfort to your life. He is the comforter and teacher of your very soul. The Bible asks you the question, have you received since you believed?"

Like a sponge, I soaked up every word. I thought, "I need joy. I need peace. I need assurance." I stayed in constant turmoil. I knew God was there. I had heard His voice, but many nights I lay in bed wondering, did He ever think about me? Does God listen as I cry out to him? Did He hear my prayers?

The Preacher spoke, "The Holy Spirit will endow you with Power." He stopped pacing and looked straight at the congregation, his eyes piercing my soul. "If you want this gift, it's yours. All you have to do is come and get it."

I had never heard of coming and getting a gift from God. It sounded like a little gift, wrapped up with a beautiful bow, just waiting for me to go and get. He made it seem so easy. I decided I would go and get this gift. How was God going to get it to me? Who would hand it to me from God? I didn't care. I was going to get it.

I stood up and made my way down the aisle toward the altar. I wept all the way because God had a gift for me. The evangelist was there to receive those who responded to the call. "Yes, come, and make your way to the altar of God. He is here to receive you."

I felt like someone drowning, needing rescued. I thought, "This is it, the turning point." It was an appointed time in my life. Finally, someone with an answer to my search had found me. This man knows something I don't know about life, about God. He's throwing me a lifeline. I walked straight to the evangelist, and he reached out his hand to receive me. "Young lady, what do you want from the Lord?"

I wiped the salty tears from my face, and thought, "How strange, he said come, and get it, and now he wants to know, what I want."

My thinking was, "Tell him you want joy, peace, assurance, and power." All I could do was look up at him with an overpowering emotion of tears. I tried to speak. I meant to say, "I want joy, peace, and assurance." Instead, a language I had never learned began to flow out of my mouth. I cleared my throat and tried again to say what I wanted, but again, a language I knew nothing about flowed like a river from deep inside me.

The evangelist started laughing. I thought, "He thinks something is wrong with me. I can't speak. Why can't I talk?" I couldn't utter one word in English.

He looked at me, "Young lady, you have received the Baptism of the Holy Spirit. Now lift your hands, and surrender to your heavenly father, and just let it flow." He turned to the rest of the people who had responded. "Those of you who are thirsty, drink from the river that will never run dry."

Leeann, who was nine years of age, and Charlie, only seven years of age, were also talking in this unknown tongue. Tears flowed down their faces. It was happening to Mother, and Pam too.

Janice was living in Jackson, Mississippi. Every Sunday morning, a neighbor would knock on her door, and invite her to church. This Sunday, Janice was dressed and ready for her. She planned to go with the lady to her church, and after the service, she would tell her she didn't like it, so the lady would just leave her alone. Unbeknownst to Janice, God had made His plans.

Janice went to church the very same day we were in the service in Montgomery and had the very same experience.

Janice called to tell us what happened to her, and we were telling her, it happened to us, too. How strange is that? How could this happen to Mom, and all five of her children, even when one child was a few hundred miles away? Can God have had this in His plan all along? Is God that big?

Everyone in our family had received this gift from God at the same time. It was a miracle. All the years of Momma's tears in the dark, crying out for God to help her, and her children, God answered in a moment. It was an appointed time for all of us. The statement that life can change on a dime is true. I don't care if you believe this, or if you have a problem with it. It's a fact. God knows I'm telling you the truth.

Lee Ann kept speaking in tongues all the way home. We undressed her and put her to bed while she cried and spoke in tongues. After Mother and I had tucked her in, I turned to Mom and asked, "Momma, do you think she will ever speak English again?"

Momma whispered, "I don't know."

We didn't know, and we didn't care. All we knew was that something had happened to all of us, something we had never heard of or understood. We just knew it was from God.

Momma and I went into the kitchen to have our coffee. I reminisced about how I had felt as though I had died and gone to heaven at that altar.

I kept saying, "Momma, He touched us." We realized that God was indeed a God of miracles.

That night, I lay in bed, crying, and talking to God. "You touched me. You touched me. For the first time in my life, you touched me." At this life-altering moment in time, it changed my life forever.

I HAVE LEARNED:

One-touch from God can go deeper than any surgeons hand, and change your life forever.
#PlasticTulips

I HAVE LEARNED:

TO TRUST IN THE LORD MEANS:

TO SLAM IT ON THE LORD

AND LEAVE IT THERE.

#PlasticTulips

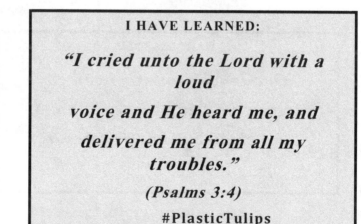

I HAVE LEARNED:

"I cried unto the Lord with a loud

voice and He heard me, and

delivered me from all my troubles."

(Psalms 3:4)

#PlasticTulips

19

He Touched Me

It was such a shock to me that I experienced the person of Jesus. No longer did I only have to know Him by faith. He touched me. I discovered that only Jesus could satisfy my soul. For the first time in my life, touched and impressed with a person that it was life changing. It was the person of Jesus. It was the person of the Holy Spirit.

I could hardly hold my pen. I was so excited when I wrote to Steve to tell him what had happened. I wondered what he would think. I had been writing love letters to Steve, but now I found another love in my life. It didn't replace Steve. This love-filled an emptiness I had inside me, and for the first time, I felt complete. Now my letters to Steve were about Jesus. After reading my Bible, I wrote to Steve, "This is for me, this is Jesus talking to me." It has introduced me to a dimension in God where His power and might is."

Steve wrote back, "Denice, what happened to you is great, but please don't write to me about religion anymore. Tell me how much you love me; how much you miss me. Tell me what you're doing during the day. Tell me about Stacy. Is she crawling? Is she walking?"

It hurt me, but I was glad he wanted to know about Stacy.

JESUS, AND THE HIPPIES

The Vietnam War was still raging. The hippie movement is taking the country by storm. Peace and Love was their message. Bob Dylan explored in country music.

On Sunday afternoons, I would go to Oak Park. It was a beautiful park, full of hippies. They called themselves flower children, with their peace, love, and anti-war slogans written on their clothes and painted on their faces. Speed, cocaine, angel dust, music, and free sex were everywhere. Some sat under trees, playing their guitars and singing while others danced. Music played on their transistor radios. The sound of confusion was in the air. No boundaries, no answers, and John Lennon singing, *"Imagine there's no heaven..."* John Lennon said the Beatles were more popular than Jesus Christ.

With my Bible in hand, I stepped up on top of a picnic table and lifted my voice as loud as I could. I shouted, "I have found the answer!" Immediately, my loud voice drew a crowd, and they began to gather around the table.

"Listen to me. Let me tell you." As I pointed, looking them straight in the eyes, I continued, "I've searched for twenty years, and now I have found the answer, God himself has touched me. You don't just have to believe there is a God. You can experience his touch, and His touch goes deep, deeper than any surgeon's hand. You look for peace and love in this world. You're not finding it because it fades. This book I have in my hand has the answer you're looking for. I met Jesus for myself. He touched me and changed my life."

One hippie in the crowd shouted, "Hey, this babe's high, man. She's tripping." Another in the crowd yelled out, "She's high on something." The crowd laughed.

Then they were getting bolder as the crowd grew. "Baby come down off that table, and I'll touch you and change your life. My touch will go deep." The crowd laughed as he did a sexual movement with his hips and hands.

I looked at him to respond, "Man, you're right. I am high. I'm high on something, and I never am going to come off. You take your drugs, tripping, but you have to come down. Then you must search for another high, a stronger high. You steal for that high. You sell yourself and your very soul for another high. And then you hit bottom. It doesn't last. In your lonely moments of hopelessness and despair, you wonder if anybody cares. You feel hopeless because you know the next fix won't fix it."

He spoke out again, "How do you know my thoughts?"

"I don't know your thoughts," I answered, "But God knows who you are. He hears every thought you have, every word, even the ones you don't speak. You wanted to kill yourself last night."

His face became almost twisted as his anger rose, turning red with rage. He shouted out with his fist in the air toward me, "Stop dipping in my Kool-Aid, you bitch!" He ran away.

I began to spend all my Sunday afternoons at the Park, spreading the Word, and then taking them with me to the evening service. I was radical and proud of it.

Plastic Tulips in the Winter

I spoke with a knowing, as the hippies and flower children listened. These were the times we were living. When the world goes through dark times, God causes light to shine. They were just like I had been—searching for answers.

I had found the answer they were looking for, and I knew it. The church people weren't excited about the way some of them came dressed, but the pastor was excited about the new faces coming in.

I tell you of this not to boast or brag but to let you know that God can take over and affect life to the point where you can't keep your mouth shut; you want everyone to know Him and His power to change a life. I'm a people lover. I was always praying to God, "Let me be a woman of knowing. I will be a voice that points them to you."

These were radical times for the world. Everyone was radical one way or the other, and I went my way. There are the silent people, in the middle people, and the grey people who stand for nothing, but that is not enjoying the journey. I had a fire in me, and I was not going to keep quiet. God had gotten under me, in me, and hold of me. And Momma too.

Momma no longer needed a psychiatrist. She had started taking hormone pills after having a hysterectomy, and her nerves were beginning to calm.

I believe it was the combination of that, and the work God was doing that started her release out of hopelessness. She was happy now and had no more bad days. She shared with people how she had tried to take her life, and they couldn't believe it.

Momma had compassion for the unlovable and the hurting. I saw the love of God in her life, and so did others. God had been listening to her as she cried alone in the dark. His eyes were on us, and we didn't even know it. I was so thankful that I had found the dimension of the Holy Spirit. He was now my teacher and guide in life. I knew I was not alone, and I never would be alone again, He walked with me and talked with me.

20

God Help Me, It Hurts

STEVE'S ACTIVE DUTY time had ended. He had served his country, and now could come home for good. When he returned this time, though, I could tell we were on two different roads in life. I knew I was going with God, with or without him.

His parents drove Stacy and me to the airport to pick him up. He stepped off the plane, and there I stood, holding Stacy. She had changed so much and didn't know her daddy. He had missed her baby stage, so she was already walking.

We took a few pictures, and then he put his sea- bag into the trunk of the car. We sat in the back seat as we headed toward the Vickers' house. They wanted Steve to spend some time with them before we went to our home. He couldn't get over how big his baby girl was. He kept hugging and kissing me.

"I'm finally home for good."

He gripped my hand the entire way, but sometimes he stared off into the distance, looking at nothing, just quiet. The radio was playing Sonny and Cher's song "Love Will Keep Us Together." It was the right song for that moment, but I knew it would take more than love to keep us together. I couldn't wait for Steve to hold me and make love to me. He was home. That's all that mattered to me.

After I put Stacy down for a nap, I began to undress. I felt shy as I slipped out of my dress, knowing Steve was sitting on the edge of the bed looking at me. "Denice, I can't touch you."

I looked at him and asked, "Steve, what's wrong?" "Denice, there's something different about you."

I responded, "Steve, I love you. That's all that matters at this moment."

He spoke up, "Wait, Denice, let me speak. When I received your letters, at first, you wrote how you couldn't wait until I held you in my arms and made love to you. You told me all the things that I needed to hear. They were building me up. I read your letters until I nearly wore the ink off the pages.

Then, suddenly, your letters changed. They were not love letters to me. They were love letters about God. Now, I've become jealous of Him. Denice, how can I compete with God? Last night, another sailor from my ship, and I got drunk. The reason I wanted to get drunk was that I knew I wanted to see you, yet part of me wanted to move as far away from you as possible.

Baby, when I got off the plane and saw you and Stacy, I wanted to run to you. You are so beautiful, but when I got close to you, I felt unworthy, unholy. I felt a presence around you, something good, and I am not good."

"Steve, I am madly in love with you. You are the love of my life. You're the man I want to spend the rest of my life. I have always thought you were the best-looking man I have ever laid my eyes on." I took his hand and placed it on my breast. "Make love to me, Steve. I've dreamed of this moment." I kissed him, and nature took its course.

That night as we were talking, I asked, "Tomorrow is Sunday, will you go to church with me?" He said he would. Partially, I suppose, because I had him over a barrel. He had just gotten home and wanted to keep me happy.

We walked into the church, and the music was loud. The choir was singing, *"I've Got A Mansion Just Over the Hill Top."* People were swaying in the aisles, clapping, and worshipping as they sang.

Steve's eyes widened. He hesitated and almost turned back toward the door. I could see the absolute terror that came upon his face.

Reverend Vaudie Lambert was the pastor, and he was on fire with a message of truth for the people. He didn't stand still when he preached but paced the platform, face red, veins popping out from his neck, and passion in his voice. The congregation was backing him up, "Amen," and "Preach it, Brother."

One thing I must say about Brother Lambert is his messages never condemned. They built up and exalted the Lord Jesus Christ. He declared what God had done for us, and how He could change our lives. I will forever be grateful to Vaudie Lambert for answering the call of God.

Steve was breathing heavily as though he could barely catch his breath. "Steve, what is wrong? Are you all right?"

He responded, "I can't breathe in this place."

Grabbing my hand, sternly, "Denice, let's get out of here." He hurried us out of the church, and we headed home.

I was discouraged; I had been hoping that Steve would like the church. When we walked into the house,

Plastic Tulips in the Winter

I was silent. I could tell he was angry. I knew a speech was coming. He went into the bedroom for a few minutes while I stayed in the kitchen. Then he came back into the room, sat down on the barstool, and spoke forcefully and direct.

"Denice, don't you ever ask me to go back to that church again. I can't breathe in that place. I don't like that church or that preacher, and I am never going back. I'll go to any other church in town, but never ask me to go back to that church."

I suppose the reason Steve was so uncomfortable was that he could sit in other churches, and not feel anything; there was no conviction. That Sunday, the presence of the Holy Spirit, which convicts us of our sins, was there. The Holy Spirit was welcome into that service, and He always shows up where He is invited

I just looked at Steve, "Okay." I could tell he was aggravated. I waited to talk about it. I certainly didn't want an argument on his first day home. After much silence and prayer on my part, I finally got up enough courage to speak.

"Steve, I'll make a deal with you. If you go back one more time, like tonight, you'll never have to enter that church door or any other church door ever again." I thought, "Oh, God, what have I just said? I've given him a reason never to go to church again. I've just fixed him for the rest of his life."

He responded, "Now, let's get this straight. If I go back tonight, you're saying you'll never speak to me about the church, God, the Bible, prayer, or any of that for the rest of our marriage?"

I took in a shallow breath as I spoke, "Yes."

He was livid. "I'll do it but know this: I'm going to hold you to it. I'll go tonight but never again."

While Steve was out to sea, I realized there were good, decent men that lived for God, and their family, so his remark didn't seem to freak me out. My mind made up. I was going to live for God. I was going to have the life God intended for me to have, even if it meant divorcing Steve. I was ready.

We arrived at the church that night, and the people had already begun to worship. Brother Lambert gave a powerful message on the changing power of God in your life. Worship music started as the pastor gave the altar call, and the choir began to sing.

"Softly, and tenderly, Jesus is calling

Calling for you and for me."

Plastic Tulips in the Winter

The pastor walked down in front of the altar. "The altar is here for you who want to receive God. Come home to God right now."

Steve jumped up from his seat. I thought he was going to run out of the building, but instead, he ran toward the altar. He ran and threw himself upon the altar, causing the rafters of the church to make a sound.

I got up from my seat, walked down the aisle, and knelt beside him. Steve slumped over the altar, on his knees. I had a flashback of our four years of marriage, and thought, "Can he go a week without lying? Can he go a month without my finding out something he has done behind my back? Will I find phone numbers in his wallet?"

I didn't believe he could. How long will this last? There is no way he can change; he is just who he is. Still, I couldn't deny what I was seeing and hearing. He was sobbing as he cried out loud, "Lord, if you still want me, I want you, but you're going to have to change me, I'm not a good person. I can't do it myself."

Later that night, Steve was so moved by what had happened to him at the altar. He wouldn't stop talking about it as we were getting ready for bed.

"Denice, as the preacher was preaching, all I could hear in my head was, You're no good. There is nothing good in me. Yet, within myself, I felt something drawing me to respond to the altar call. I knew it was now or never. Denice, when I fell in love with you, I was attracted at first to your looks, but then I saw something deeper in you. You had a hunger for more in life, for everything pure and right in life. I have had no right to your love. I was ruining your life and our love. I knew I was doing what people said I would do to you. I've tried to hold on to you, and yet I've lived in filth on the other hand. Baby, you have been my only contact with goodness in this world. I told the Lord, if you still want me, I want you, but you're going to have to change me. I told Him I would give him my life."

"Steve, God is transforming you into the man you are meant to be. What happened at the altar is real."

21

Never Touch Me Again

DURING THE NEXT few weeks, Steve experienced regeneration in his life. He wanted all of God he could have. His started a new job going door-to-door selling life insurance. Right away, it seemed that all he could see was their need for Jesus and praying for them.

Weeks passed, and I noticed I didn't see any cigarette ashes in the ashtrays. Steve had been a chain smoker, going through one to two packs a day. There was always a cigarette in his mouth. But I noticed all the ashtrays were clean. "Steve, where are you putting all your cigarette ashes?"

He looked up from reading his Bible, smiled, "You know, I just quit desiring cigarettes."

He had tried to quit many times before and hadn't succeeded, but now the habit was gone. That addiction was taken from him with ease and no struggle. Smoking isn't a sin; it won't send you to hell. Your clothes will just smell like you have been there.

I began to see other changes in Steve. God was moving swiftly in his life. I woke up at night and would hear him praying in "unknown tongues," seeking the face of God.

Our lives were changing. We began hanging out with other couples from the church. Things were going along too well for anything to be wrong again, or so I thought. I had one more dreadful lesson to learn, and it would tear right at the core of my being.

Several months of joy swept over us after Steve's commitment of his life to Christ. For the first time in our marriage, it appeared I was free. I had peace, and a feeling of contentment, together, we pursued our relationship with God.

LISTEN TO HIM

One night, Steve had been quiet and came into the bedroom to talk to me. I was dressing for the midweek service. I could always tell when Steve had something on his mind—he starts to bite the corner of his lip.

"Denice, sit down. I want to tell you something." The aggressive undertone in his voice sounded as if he were going to tell me something he did not want to say, but something God was forcing him to get it out.

Plastic Tulips in the Winter

My mind began to say, "Oh no, he's going to admit things to you. You don't want him to tell you anything. You don't want this bubble around you to burst. You don't want him to say a word. Stop him, stop him. You like things the way they are. God, please don't let him confess anything to me. Let me live in this realm of total happiness, peace, and joy. God, just tell Steve that we've begun a new life, and to forget the past. I don't want to hear it."

I then heard this still small voice say, "Denice, listen to him. Hear him out. You can take it. Let Steve be free for the last time, once, and for all. I will see you through this." I stood to listen.

"Denice, I'm going to tell you something. When I tell you, I know you're going to take Stacy, and you're going to leave me. I know you, Denice. I've got to get this off my chest. I can't go on like this. I want to walk in total freedom with nothing to hide. I'm not going to live any longer with the threat of my past. I'm going forward in my future with God, so I've got to tell you."

Steve had reason to be worried because I had told him that if I ever caught him with another woman, there would never be a second chance. One strike, and you're out. I was not going to be any man's doormat.

He continued, "Denice, I've weighed the cost, and I've thought this through. I know that no matter what happens, I've got to go all the way with God. You might as well know, this sounds hard, but I've got to walk with God first, even above you, and Stacy. Even if it means I lose both of you. It's not what I want to happen, but I know how I can mess my life up. From now on, I'm doing it God's way."

He continued, "The entire four years that I have lived with you, I have been lying to you. I have lied to cover up lies. I was going out to drinking parties and getting drunk, while you thought I was on night duty. His lips quivered, and he had tears in his eyes. "Denice, I have committed adultery."

He told me of the times and places. I watched the expression on his face. His lips were trembling as he spoke. I could see the suffering as he tried to relieve himself of this pain. I knew all along that there were times Steve had lied to me, but when the word adultery came out of his lips, it was as though he had just plunged a knife deep into my gut and turned it. I felt dead inside.

Steve looked at me, waiting for me to scream, yell, cry, throw a fit, or show some emotion, but there was nothing there. I couldn't even feel anger. My marriage with Steve Vickers died at that moment. It was over. He waited for my reply, but I was silent. I only looked at him and lifted my hand for him to keep his distance.

"Steve, I've heard every word you just said. I don't know what I'm going to do about what you've just told me. But, don't you come near me; the thought of you touching me makes me want to vomit. You will never touch me ever again. I can't live with you anymore; all I want right now is you out of my sight."

If God had opened a hole in the earth that led to the fiery furnace, I would have kicked him in it. I felt nothing for him. I was in my own pain. I felt life was only going to hurt me. You, the reader, must understand, we are but flesh, we hurt, we feel the pain, and still need God to see us through.

Steve slept in the other bedroom. In the middle of the night, he came into my room and softly touched me to wake me. "Denice, Denice," his voice was just above a whisper, as he trembled, "Pray for me. God can't forgive such great sin."

He was on the floor on his knees, crying with his head buried into the side of the mattress. He was asking me to pray for him, but I didn't love him anymore. I didn't care, I wanted to say to him, Jesus just phoned, and He said He hates you, after all.

I knew my attitude was wrong, and that I had to care about the anguish he was in and should pray over him, so I did. Deep down I cared that he got peace in his soul.

I placed my hand on his head, "God, show Steve that he is saved and that you have forgiven him." At the same time, I heard a voice say to me, "But you can't forgive him." I knew God was right. I knew he needed a touch from God. I wanted him to have God, but I didn't want Steve to have any part of me. However, I continued laying my hands on his head and praying for him. "God, show Steve, you can forgive such great sin." I was hurting in my own pain.

Steve returned to the other room to sleep. I'd wake up in the middle of the night and hear him praying. His prayers could be heard throughout the house. I would see Steve reading his Bible. My feeling of nothingness for him turned to more anger, and the anger turned to pain. I was mad because men were always flirting with me, but I was never tempted. I didn't deserve this from a man. For three nights in a row, this scene repeated itself: Steve came into my bedroom, woke me, and cried, "Denice, pray for me. God can't forgive such great sin."

Plastic Tulips in the Winter

All my mind could see was Steve with the other women. As I cleaned the house, I would become sick to my stomach and throw up in the toilet. I soon discovered three things that would save me from this hurt: reading the Bible, playing Christian music in the house, and praying. Without doing one of these things, I was left alone in my mind tormented.

####

One night, I was in agony. I couldn't stop thinking about his adultery, so I called Pam. I was crying out of control, "Pam, I'm dying. Pam, is there such a thing as dying of a broken heart?"

She answered me, "I don't know, Denice," as she, too, started sobbing over my pain.

I told her, "If there is, I'm telling you, I'm dying Pam. I'm dying." My scream was loud, and my pain was deep. Pam and I cried together. "Pam, Daddy, did this to us, and now my husband is doing this to me. I'm tired of this, Pam. I am so tired of this pain.

All she could say was, "Denice, I know, I know. "She cried. She moaned in pain for my pain. We were like two little girls crying together.

I'M HURTING

The next morning as I was vacuuming the living room, my mind raced with pictures of Steve with other women. I turned the vacuum cleaner off, threw myself on the living room carpet, and buried my face in my hands.

I screamed, and it echoed throughout the house, "God, help me! Help me, God. It hurts. It hurts. I'm hurting. I'm hurting.!" I screamed out like a madwoman, "God, please let me out of this marriage! I don't love him anymore!"

Suddenly God's presence filled the room. It was as if He stood at attention when I called on Him. From an inward voice, I heard, "Denice, if you will see this man through this, I will give you the man you never dreamed you could have."

I talked back, "God, you give me a man I never dreamed I could have, but don't let his name be Steve Vickers. I don't love him anymore," I cried.

The Holy Spirit spoke back to me, "This man." I had heard His voice. I got up and continued to clean the house. I knew He was saying, "This man."

Later that day, I realized that I was no longer hurting. The house seemed peaceful. I realized I wasn't being tormented in my mind, about Steve. I laid across my bed, flat on my back. I lay there, trying to imagine Steve in bed with another woman. It didn't hurt. I made it kinky, dirty, and in color. I could see it in my mind, but it still didn't hurt. "Lord, what's going on? It's supposed to hurt. Why doesn't it hurt?"

I heard God within me say, "You said it hurts. So, I took the pain away." I questioned him back. "You can take the pain away?" All my life, I have had this pain inside of me. First, Daddy, and now, Steve. Now, at the age of twenty, I'm finding out that He can take hurt away. I was changed in a moment. I made a choice to listen to His voice. He took the hurt away.

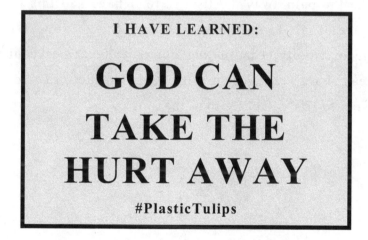

I HAVE LEARNED:

GOD CAN TAKE THE HURT AWAY

#PlasticTulips

22

He Does Not Deserve
Your Love

STEVE CAME HOME from work and sat down in the living room to read. I walked past him as I went to cook dinner and thought, "He is so handsome." His dark eyes, brown hair, and mustache always took my breath away. I told myself not to look at him, but I wanted to look at him again. I walked toward the bedroom and glanced back. I thought, "Look how handsome he looks, sitting in that chair, reading his Bible. I don't want to look. What's wrong with you? You're getting attracted to him again. Don't look at him. He doesn't deserve your love. "

I felt like a schoolgirl again, seeing him for the first time. I felt myself being drawn to him, and I became afraid that he would notice. I didn't want to start loving him again, but I couldn't help it. It all happened so fast. It was a whirlwind.

Steve had been a gentleman during those weeks when I had nothing to say or do with him. I was in pain. He had not forced himself upon me; instead, he had continued to seek God. The passion started to build within me. I knew God had said to me that He took my pain away. I walked over to the chair and knelt beside him. "Steve, I love you, and I want you to move back into the bedroom."

He choked back the tears, hesitated for a moment, "Denice, are you sure? If I move back into that bedroom, I'm never going to leave it ever again. Are you sure, Denice? Are you sure this is what you want?" I replied. "Yes, I'm sure."

Three voices were speaking, the enemy of my soul, God's voice, and my voice. I had to choose which voice to listen to. God's voice was saying, "See this man through this." The enemy of my soul said," "He does not deserve your love," and my voice was saying, "I'm hurting."

I had a choice; I choose to believe God's voice. I used my voice and said, "I'm sure." My voice was the third voice to make a choice. It is a powerful voice. It's a weapon, CHOICE. Our choice in agreement with God is powerful. A weapon in our warfare.

The moment was serene. Our eyes met as if for the first time, and I knew we were in love with each other. I looked into Steve's eyes, and all I could see was the truth. I was no longer looking for a green thread. He was not going to be the man like my daddy, with plastic tulips, and nothing real.

There would be no plastic tulips to fool people. I saw what I was going to have as a husband. I didn't have to wonder anymore. I knew for the first time in my life that God had given me a man I never dreamed I could have. I had been married to Steve for four years, and it was as if I was looking at him for the first time. We were free for the first time. We were both free from our past.

Action does not always bring happiness, but there is no happiness without action. I read once that a foolish man seeks happiness in the future. The wise man grows it under his feet.

My earthly father only showed up in my life every few years to hurt me, to tell me what a rotten kid I was, and to show off his latest conquest.

I HAVE LEARNED:

Action does not always

bring happiness.

BUT

There is no happiness

without action.

#PlasticTulips

I HAVE LEARNED:

A Foolish man seeks happiness

in the future.

BUT

The Wise man grows it

under his Feet.

#PlasticTulips

23

Get Out Of Town

I APPLIED FOR a job as an orthodontic assistant. At the interview, I told the doctor that I didn't have a high school diploma. I also told him I was not trained in orthodontics, but that I loved to be around teenagers. I assured him I was a quick learner, and that I'd bring fun to his office. "I'm a party waiting to happen, and teens need someone like me around when they come to your office to get their braces checked." I smiled and added, "You won't regret training me. "

The whole time I was talking, he was smiling at me. He stopped me in the middle of a sentence, "You're hired."

After a few weeks of working, I explained to my boss I had a family problem. He asked me if there was anything, he could do to help me. I told him; I had just found out my dad was running a black prostitution house downtown. I was going to go shut him down.

He said he was sorry I had such a disappointing father. I looked down and responded, "I know."

I drove down the street to a neighborhood I knew to be rough. I knew not to drive into that area because of all the shootings and drug problems. I was in my early twenties, a white girl at that, who had no business around that part of town.

The old wooden shack houses had porches falling apart with broken down sofas and recliner chairs sitting on the porches. Cars were jacked up in the yard, no tires on them, and grass growing all around.

I pulled up in front of the address that was given to me by an informer. There were two black girls in sheer lingerie sitting on the porch swing. "Hi, Sugar, what you want?"

"Is Charles Perkins here?"

"Just a minute, Shug." She walked over to the screen door and yelled, "Charlie, there's a young girl here to see ya." She then walked over to an old, rotting white column, leaned her back against it, and propped one foot up against the column. She was checking me out while the other girl filed her fingernails, never looking up at me.

"He be here in a minute."

Plastic Tulips in the Winter

He was forty-five, dressed in black dress pants, a white starched shirt with the sleeves rolled up and no tie. As he looked through the screen door and pushed it open, there was no smile. He didn't like that I had found him there. He stepped out onto the porch and asked, "What do you want?"

"Daddy, I heard you have this house you're running, and I know you still work for JSH Company. Leeann and Charlie are still in elementary school. I don't want them to know what you're doing. I'm giving you twenty-four hours to clear out of town. If you don't, I'm going to your job, and then to the police to tell them about these prostitutes, and you."

He didn't say a word. He just had a blank look on his face as he turned to go into the house.

He moved to Jasper, Alabama that night.

MY MAN

I went home to a man whose life was being transformed. I wanted to believe that I could believe in this man. That he could be trusted. The Holy Spirit began to teach me how to treat a man. He would tell me things to say to Steve.

One morning, he was in the bathroom shaving. I turned him around to face me with his face all lathered up.

I looked him straight in the eyes, "Steve, I really do love you."

He looked as if he questioned it and asked, "Do you, Denice?"

I could see his questioning eyes, so I again said, "Steve, I really do love you."

God began to teach Steve and me about tender words and tender touch toward each other. Steve was caught up in the freedom he was experiencing in God. The change in him influenced Momma and my sisters.

Life was good. Steve and I both ran after God and each other. I loved the man he was becoming. I let God teach me how to love and treat a man. Peace and happiness prevailed in our house.

24

Fast Into The Future

WEDNESDAY NIGHT while I was at choir practice, Steve sat in the back of the church talking with Pastor Lambert. He was weeping, telling him, "If I could do anything for the rest of my life, it would be preaching the gospel. I want to help the hurting, broken, and bruised of life, and tell them of the goodness of God."

Pastor Lambert prayed with Steve, "Son, that's the call of God on your life. Just say, 'Yes' to God."

After choir practice, Brother Lambert said, "Denice, it looks like you, and Steve will be leaving us to go to Bible College." Immediately, I remembered when I was fourteen years old sweeping the carpet, and I had heard God speak to me and say, "You're going to be married to a preacher." It was God's plan, and my destiny as He watched over me.

We knew it was time to tell Steve's parents. Steve dreaded the reaction he would get from his dad. His dad had grand plans for him as a lawyer. Steve was then to go into politics.

Steve felt he never measured up to his father's expectations. His daddy would say, "One of the most valuable things in life is when you walk down the street and hear people say, 'There goes Steve Vickers."

Steve and his family always had everything first class. Vick, Steve's father had the precise appearance of a Southern gentleman. He wore a white suit, and he walked with a black cane that had a brass handle. His hair and mustache were white, and he had deep blue eyes. I pictured that's how Steve would look because he was built just like his daddy.

Vick and Nettie always retired to their master suite to watch TV after dinner. Their bedroom door was open, so we walked in. His daddy, as usual, was sitting in his chair, smoking his pipe. He looked so distinguished in his black silk smoking jacket. Nettie was sitting up in bed while they both watched The Lawrence Welk Show.

"Momma, and Daddy, I want to share my plans with you. I'm going to be a minister." Steve looked at his dad to see his response.

Plastic Tulips in the Winter

His father's head dropped down in irritation, biting his bottom lip in disappointment. Steve and I knew a speech was coming.

He looked at Steve as he spoke. "Son, you know there's no money in that. How will you provide for your family? Son, you must focus on success, and how you are going to get there. Not this religious stuff."

Steve replied, "Dad, I don't care about money. I want to spend my life helping people. Dad, God has called me." The air was filled with tension; his dad was frustrated.

Trying to calm the situation, his mother spoke up, "That's wonderful, son. I hear Samford in Birmingham is a great Bible College." I could tell Steve's parents were ashamed we were Pentecostals.

"Mother, that might be so, but I think that the Lord wants me to go to Southeastern Bible College in Lakeland, Florida." We knew he could get his BA in theology there.

"Okay, son," she spoke gently.

His daddy spoke up, "Your mother, and I love you, and we want you to be happy." Then he locked his jaw in disapproval, adding, "But if you're going to be a damn preacher, you better be the best damn preacher there is."

"Yes, sir."

Deep down, I did respect his dad. We were alike in many ways. I had a strong drive for spiritual things and he in natural. I also think we both lacked balance in the natural and the spiritual.

We moved to Lakeland, Florida, in January 1972 so Steve could get his degree. We spent the next three years working hard getting through college. Steve already had a year of college credits from the University of Alabama. I worked as an orthodontic assistant, and Stacy was in daycare at our church.

Once settled into work and school, we began to meet other couples in college. Friday nights, we had married couples over for a bag of Taco Bell and a movie. Every couple lived on a tight budget. I made Momma's fudge, and it was a hit.

I must tell you I did have a day as I was vacuuming the apartment a need to ask Steve questions and rehash information of the adultery.

Plastic Tulips in the Winter

I instantly felt sick at my stomach. That same old feeling of emotional, mental pain was there. The Holy Spirit, the voice of God, spoke to me, "Run to me."

Then He said, "Let this be your thermostat, every time you feel or think these thoughts, run to me. Take my peace."

CHILDREN OF FAITH

Mom was invited to be a housemother with a mission team in the Dominican Republic. She had spent her adult life trying to clothe, and feed five children, and just keep the power on. She was so tired of working, and it sounded like heaven to her. She and I talked about the fact that Leeann didn't want to go, but mom thought it could be a great life experience. I told mom if Leeann didn't like it there, send her home to me.

She took Charlie and Leeann, but Leeann only stayed a week.

Here I was only twenty-one, and Steve twenty-five, raising a toddler, and now a teenager. She was a typical teenage girl, into make-up and fashion. She was blessed with Mom's thick brown hair and had a cute little figure. We were able to put her in a Christian school on a scholarship program. She was gifted in her ability to take over any school project. Whether it was decorating the school for Christmas, organizing school parties, or handling any project given to her; she took it over, and was a natural. Leeann was also a natural cook. It wasn't unusual for me to come home from work to a fully cooked meal. That was great.

Steve and I laid in bed at night, laughing about Leeann, and praying to God for wisdom on parenting a teenager. We were young ourselves. We prayed together for Leeann to be confident and happy with us. She was very respectful to us, which made it easy.

After two years in the Dominican Republic, Mom and Charlie returned to the states and moved to Lakeland to live near us. He loved it in the Dominican. He learned to speak Spanish, and they loved Charlie's blonde curls. He stood out in the crowd.

Leeann moved back in with Mom, and we all attended the same church together. Then Daddy paid a visit.

He called Mom and said he wanted to see them. She told him he could come. She felt it might be right for Leeann, and Charlie to see him since he had left when they were babies. He was going to stay at Mom's house in Leeann's room, and Leeann would sleep with Mom.

It was going to be a short visit. We thought God was going to do something in Daddy. Maybe He would put the family back together. We believed God could change a life, and we were hoping this would be it for Daddy.

He arrived on Friday. The next day, Mom had to go to the Laundromat to wash clothes because the apartment she lived in didn't have a washer and dryer hook up. Charlie stayed home with Daddy.

Dad had never given us any reason not to trust him around Charlie. Dad's problems had always been with women. Charlie ran to the Laundromat, sobbing, and told Mom that Daddy had molested him. He was twelve years old. He told Momma everything that had happened, and it knocked the wind out of her. She called Steve to come over. Steve told Daddy to get his things and get out. Steve wanted to beat the living hell out of him, but I kept him from doing it.

Charlie was just a boy, an innocent child. He longed for his daddy, and this is what his father did. It is not a child's fault when an adult takes advantage of them. Remember, this was the 1970s.

If it had happened in this day and time 2020, we would have called the police. A lot came out after this happened. We talked about everything Dad did in front of us as children and learned Janice had been a victim. He showed up when she was seventeen and had just gotten a divorce from her teenage marriage. Daddy asked if she would have sex with his brother. She didn't, but she hated him for that. It made her feel cheap. She said if he died, she would not go to his funeral.

Steve graduated from college and was named the salutatorian. The week after graduation, I gave birth to our second daughter, Misty Shae. Stacy was five years old and wanted us to name her new baby sister Ronald McDonald. I assured her Misty Shae was a better name.

We went on staff as Youth Pastors of our home church in Montgomery, Alabama, under Pastor Frank Martin of Evangel Temple.

A year later, Steve felt the direction of God to start traveling as an evangelist, holding revivals in churches across the country. We bought a used twenty-eight-foot travel trailer and pulled it behind our van.

Steve was driving the vehicle, a trailer in tow, and I was reading out loud the life story of Smith Wigglesworth. He was a man who believed in God and saw miracles. He had stepped out in faith, and God did miracles in his services.

Steve began to weep. He pulled off the side of the road, got out of the car, and walked over onto the grass.

Plastic Tulips in the Winter

At first, I didn't know where he was going. Steve stood beside the car on the interstate with his hands lifted toward heaven, crying, "God, I believe in you. God, let me see miracles, use me, God. Use me for your glory."

I was sitting in the car, crying too. I knew that God wanted us to be children of faith. I also realized how powerful our God was. I began to see that God was as big as we let Him be in our lives. Steve opened the car door, sat down, and looked at me. "I believe in God. I am not going to settle for less. I'm going to see God move in me and use me. I'm going to see blind eyes opened, and the deaf will hear. I will see the lame walking, and the captives set free. I'm going to tell them of God's love and mercy. That God will change their lives and bless them if they will only cry out to Him. I'm going to tell them God is faithful, and that God cares about their every need. Denice, are you with me?"

I shouted out, "I'm with you, Steve!"

I knew that he was going to see these things in his ministry. I thought back to the day when we were youth pastors, and I was walking down the stairs and noticed Steve sitting in his chair reading the Bible. God stopped me at the foot of the stairs and asked me a question, "Do you see that man over there?"

I replied, "Lord, you know, I see that, man."

He responded, "He is not yours; He is mine; I'm just lending him to you." Steve and I did follow God. I watched Steve in services as God powerfully used him. I knew it was all God, and that Steve was the empty vessel filled with God, desiring to be used by Him.

We were a voice for God. We let people know that if they cried out to Him for help; He would step into their life in a minute and turn things around. Our lives were proof. We could say, look at us. Many times, I was reminded of the Scripture, "To whom much is given, much is required" (Luke 12:48). We were sold out to God.

Many times, Steve's daddy had a look of disappointment toward us because the ministry was not his idea of success. He removed Steve from the family's will. He was unhappy with the direction Steve had taken in his life. I would tell Steve, "If he gets saved, I will be able to believe for anybody."

It wasn't long, and Steve's dad came down with terminal cancer. He told us he was listening to a TV preacher named Charles Stanley.

Plastic Tulips in the Winter

We began to see a change in him. He softened and was open to talking about God. This man used to cuss out the TV preachers as he changed the channel. He'd yell at the television, "That damn preacher! All they want is my money."

We asked God to let us know without a doubt that he would spend eternity in heaven. A few nights before Vick died, the hospital called for us to come. They told us that Vick had been asking for me. He kept asking, "When is she coming?"

I walked over to his bedside. He looked at me, smiled, and put his hand out toward me as I placed my hand in his. "You made it," and folded his hand with mine.

"Denice, I want you to forgive me. You were right, and I was wrong." He spoke this in front of all his loved ones. This man has never admitted he was wrong about anything. He continued, "Now I understand everything you ever told me about God. I want you, and Steve to know I am proud of you, and keep up the good work that you are doing."

His feelings had changed toward his son, but he didn't have time to put Steve back in the will. He never left the hospital.

####

We were homeschooling Stacy, who was in the second grade, while we traveled. I was ready for us to get settled, so I told Steve I wanted us to buy a home, and let Stacy go to public school for the third grade. Steve was still traveling, preaching from church to church. We bought a house.

One day Steve was relaxing, reading a book our bedroom, and I had just stepped out of the shower.

As I stood naked in front of the mirror brushing my long, dark hair, I stared at myself and realized how much I had changed and grown over the years. I had married Steve when I was only sixteen, and now, I was twenty-seven. I walked over to him, and he looked up from his book and asked, "What?"

"Steve, looking in the mirror, I just realized when you married me, I was a little girl. I'm not a little girl anymore. I'm a woman."

Steve smiled, "I knew this day would come. I have always thought you were the most beautiful woman I have ever seen. Denice, I thought if you ever saw yourself the way others see you; you might not stay with me. You would think you could do better."

Plastic Tulips in the Winter

"Better? Steve Vickers, get in that bed, and let me show you what this woman wants." We had a craving for each other. It was sexual, emotional, spiritual, and it was beautiful. It was a love affair between two people, body, mind, and soul, completely given to each other—living for each other, and both living for God. You can't get any stronger or better in this life than that.

Steve's Parents

Cecil and Nettie Lou Vickers

25

The Spirit Of The Lord

O NE MORNING while I was getting Stacy ready for the school bus, I noticed Misty was not out of bed. She was usually a rambunctious five-year-old. "Misty, don't you want to get up and have some breakfast with Stacy."

She didn't move. I walked over and felt her forehead. She was burning with fever. "Misty, get up, baby. I'm going to take you to see a doctor."

She couldn't walk. I picked her up, laid her in the back seat of the car with Stacy, and drove her to the doctor's office. The doctor, immediately realizing she was unable to walk and had a fever with extreme fatigue, requested bloodwork.

The doctor said, "Mrs. Vickers, we need to hospitalize Misty to see what we are dealing with."

Within hours of being in the hospital, I informed Misty had Osteomyelitis, an inflammation of the bone in her right leg. It was a form of cancer. The doctors began to talk to me about possible amputation. They said that the disease had already eaten through the growth plate of her leg, and the diseased bone must be removed along with tissue around it to stop it from spreading. It could mean death if they didn't move fast.

I called Steve, who was out of town, and he canceled his meetings and rushed home. Misty was in the hospital for ten days with IV treatments of antibiotics given around the clock before considering removing her leg.

Sitting up all night in the hospital not being able to sleep, I was suffocating with fear. I was overwhelmed with the thought of possible amputation or death for my five-year-old. I sat beside her bed with my hand on her leg, crying all night.

All I could say out loud was, "Now God, now God." I felt like someone was holding a pillow over my mouth. I could hardly breathe. I knew only God could turn this around. Daily, the doctors discussed with us amputation, but my mind was made up: not my daughter.

Plastic Tulips in the Winter

While in prayer, God told Steve that not one bone would be broken. Steve and I switched out the next morning. While he sat with her, I went home to freshen up.

Sitting in the bathtub, I cried, asking God, "Why? Why God? We have dedicated our lives to you. We are spending our lives serving you, why, God?"

I heard that inner voice speaks, *"When the enemy comes in like a flood, the Spirit of the Lord will raise up a standard against him."* (Isaiah 59:19).

I jumped out of the tub like a madwoman. That's all I needed, a word from God. I drove as fast as I could to the hospital to tell Steve. I threw open the door of her hospital room, pointed at Steve, and declared, "When the enemy comes in like a flood, the Spirit of the Lord will raise up a standard against him."

Steve jumped up was and began to dance around, saying, "Yes! Yes! Yes!"

We got our miracle. The doctors did not amputate. I am telling you, one word from God mixed with our faith turned things around.

We didn't have medical insurance, and the hospital bill was going to be over a hundred thousand dollars. I was sitting in the hospital room when the door opened slightly, and a blonde headed woman with the most beautiful smile was poking her head around the door. Without stepping into the room, "I'm a representative. Go to the Cripple Children's Clinic. They are waiting for you to sign the papers. They will pay your bills." Then she left.

I told Steve what happened. "Let's go."

When we arrived at the Cripple Children's Clinic, I explained to them that their representative came by and told me to come to sign some papers. They said they had no one who does that. I looked at all the desks and couldn't find her. The lady was amazed at my story. She came back into her office with the forms for us to sign. Our medical debt was cleared.

We checked Misty out of the hospital, and as the double doors opened for us to exit, I turned to Steve and asked, "Do we have the victory?"

He responded, "Yes, we have the victory."

We began to know what the taste of sweet, sweet victory, taste like.

We looked down at our Misty walking between us, healed, and no medical bills to pay. We had a taste of victory in our mouths. There is nothing like that taste of sweet, sweet, sweet victory.

Plastic Tulips in the Winter

Misty's leg was not supposed to grow because it had eaten through the growth plate, but it grew just as her other leg grew. She would one day become a physical trainer with the most perfect body you have ever laid your eyes on. The doctor wrote across his medical records, Unexplainable phenomenon. God is good.

####

In 1980 Pam got a divorce. She did not want a divorce, but her husband did. She moved back to Montgomery with her three children. She asked, "Who is going to want me with three little children?"

Even as beautiful as she was, I, too, wasn't sure what man would want her with three little children. I knew sharing my concern would not bring her comfort. I told her she could trust God, and I shared Romans 8:38 with her, "And we know that God causes all things to work together for the good for those who are called according to His purpose." I told her, "Pam, you can trust God."

She nodded her head as she softly responded, "I will."

Pam was always burying her face in her Kleenex. She was an umbrella and handkerchief person. She was funny like that. I'm neither. I would rather get rained on and look for Kleenex when I need one. Isn't that funny how different we were? We made each other laugh.

Janice, now with four sons, and single again, ended up back in Montgomery also. I laughed, and told Momma, "Isn't it something, all these single women in churches go to the altar praying and believing God for a husband, and Janice can marry as many men as she wants." Men just loved Janice, and Janice sure liked men. The key for her, I guess, was how she made men feel about themselves.

Janice had gone through the hippie movement, smoking weed, going to Woodstock, the whole nine yards, trying it all. She would go to the Copa Club in her white patent knee-high boots, and short, fitted mini dress. They always let Janice be one of the girls dancing in a cage. Remember, she wanted to grow up and be a heart surgeon or a go-go girl in a cage. Well, there you go. Isn't that funny how life is?

Now, here we all were back in Montgomery together with Momma. Leeann, and Charlie, who were now teenagers. We were all going to the same church and trusting God to teach us and show us our way through life. You can see we were not perfect people, and life wasn't perfect, but we ran after a perfect God.

Plastic Tulips in the Winter

HAVE YOU FLIRTED TODAY?

One afternoon, I met Pam for lunch, and just as we were leaving the office where she worked, a young man with dark hair and a dark mustache walked by us, "Pam, I will see you after lunch."

"Wow, who in the world is that?" I asked.

"My boss," she answered.

I responded, "You got to be kidding me. You have worked for him for two years now. All this time, I knew your boss was single, but you never told me he looked like that. I figured he was old and unattractive, but he is gorgeous. I would throw that man down on the ground and lay my lips on top of his mustache."

Pam laughed, "He is dating someone."

"Pam, that doesn't mean you can't move in on this. Has he put a ring on her finger?" "No."

"Then, all is fair in love and war. I'll help you catch him. "She just laughed at me as I talked.

I began to instruct her on flirting. She responded as she giggled, "Denice, I haven't flirted in years, I've forgotten how."

As we sat at lunch, I went over flirting instructions. I was giving Pam my expertise on flirting. We both laughed at my way of catching a man.

Every day I called her to ask, "Have you flirted with him today?"

She whispered over the office phone, "I don't think he got that I was flirting." I had to work with her on that. We got a lot of laughs out of me, teaching Pam how to flirt.

Eventually, he took the bait, and they married and had two more daughters to add to her two sons and daughter. That made five. I call that "Woman Power."

I just have that push in me. If I want it, it's mine. I just must figure out how to get it.

26

Christian Life Church

WE COULD SENSE a change was coming in our lives. We didn't know what it was, but there was something in the air. We loved how God was using us to affect the lives of people at each of the churches, but at the same time, we were ready for Steve to stop traveling.

One night, while Steve was preaching out of town, I prayed asking God what He wanted us to do. "God, if you will just tell me what your will is, we will do it. We only want to be in your perfect will." I fell asleep while repeatedly asking, "What do you want us to do? What do you want us to do?"

The next morning, I awoke to the sound of the telephone ringing. "Hello?"

The voice on the other end of the telephone was a woman's voice. "You don't know me, and I don't know you, but as I was in prayer this morning, God gave me your phone number. He instructed me to ask you a question."

My first thought was, I've got some flake on the phone. I had never heard of God giving a phone number to anyone. "Okay, what is the question God has?"

She answered, "He said to ask you, *'What do you want?'"* She instantly had my attention.

She continued, "I'm to hang up and let you tell Him."

I had fallen asleep the night before while asking God to tell me what He wanted us to do, and now, He is asking me what I want. I knew this was God.

"Woman, you have heard from God." I hung up.

I never thought about what I might want. We lived life through prayer and obedience. The vital question now was, what do I want? I laid there, and then took a step of faith, and spoke out loud, "I, Denice Vickers, want Steve Vickers to pastor in Montgomery, Alabama." I was amazed at what came out of my mouth. I backed it up with be a "dad-gum."

Plastic Tulips in the Winter

The Bible says it's within you; just ask me for it. I was learning God's destiny and will for our life. I called Steve and told him what had happened. It wasn't long before we had our first church service in our living room with Momma, Leeann, Kenny, Charlie, Janice, Pam, a dentist, and his wife, two young single brothers, Norris, and Wayne Braswell, my Avon lady, and of course, all our children. That was the birth of Christian Life Church in August 1980.

One month later, we moved into a tiny rented church building. Our first Sunday in that building, I told Steve I knew how we would know that the hand of God was on us to be a pastor. The sign would be if God sends a Black family to our church, and they choose us as their pastors. Remember this was in the 1980s. You would never see that in the South—Blacks and Whites attending church together. At our first Sunday service, Sam, and Willa Carpenter, a handsome Black couple, walked in.

I turned to Steve and said, "Now, let's have church."

The first year of the church, the neighbor who had taken my dad from us, Marie, came to a Sunday morning service. I wondered how she could come; knowing Momma and all her kids would be at the service. There was no way Marie did not know I was married to the pastor. I knew she came with a purpose. I had always felt if I had the opportunity to tell her off, I would take it.

She answered the altar call. I walked over to her and asked her, "What do you want me to pray with you about?" She put her hand on her chest, "My heart."

I knew she wasn't talking about heart trouble, but that her heart hurt for what she had done. A scripture came to mind: "Until I make your enemies a footstool for your feet." (Luke 20:43) I knew right then I could wipe my feet on her, or I could give her mercy. I chose to give her mercy. I pointed at Momma and all her children and said, "Because of God, we survived, and we are blessed by God. You go now and suffer no more; we are all right." I prayed for her, and she left. I never saw her again.

I was amazed at how God brought her to me. He wanted to allow me to wipe my feet on her, but He knew I would give her mercy. Isn't God something? He knows us.

As I write about this with 70 knocking at my door. I look back on that moment, that room, Marie and Mom. Momma was shaken being in the same room with Marie and did not walk over to say anything. I realize now I was a different woman. Confident at the moments of CHOICE. That's not to put Mom down in any way. The struggles of my life, instead of shaking my world, had made me stronger.

SEEK THE FATHER

One night in my sleep, God spoke to me, *"Seek the Father as hard as the Father is seeking you."* I woke up, sat up in bed, and pointed to Steve, who was sitting in a chair reading his Bible. I quoted to him what I had was told in my sleep. Then I put my hand on my chest, "All my life, I saw myself as running hard after God. I never knew He was running hard after me."

For twenty-five years, Steve, and I preached to thousands. Steve was a man of prayer. It was normal for our children to fall asleep while hearing their daddy pray out loud to God for guidance. His hunger to feed the people the Word of God was real and passionate. We took every service with absolute seriousness. We knew you never have the same people in each service. We also knew that people walk in with thoughts of divorce, pain, and overall sadness. We were the voice God had sent them to hear.

I tell you these things not to boast of us, but to prove to you He is God, and He, will help those who cry out to Him and call Him Lord. We were two imperfect people who believed in a perfect God.

We made a great team, but without God, Steve, and I knew we would be nothing. We walked, lived, and breathed, telling people how big God was.

John Osteen, the father of the now well-known Joel Osteen, was a pastor that we looked to for guidance early on in our years of ministry. He, and his wife, Dodie, took the time to mentor Steve and me. John Osteen once told us that if we built a fire, people would come to warm by it. We knew what he meant. All we had to do was be on fire with the Word of God, burning with the message of His saving power.

People came, and they responded because we had a fire in our belly, knowing in us that we had found the answer. We were going to shout it to those who had ears to hear. Only God could fill that space. We knew there was nothing exceptional about Steve, and Denice without His anointing.

I would hear God ask me, *"Denice, what do you know?"* I would say back to Him, "I know you!" I knew I didn't know much, but I felt I understood what was important in this life. The Bible says, "What does it profit a man if he gains the whole world but loses his soul?"

Plastic Tulips in the Winter

Steve, being a man's man and a strong leader, spoke with passion and conviction. He made straight A's in college. They say opposites attract. I guess in this matter, it was true. Steve liked me just the way I was.

Momma, Janice, Pam, and their spouses were always sitting in the audience, listening to Steve or me speak. Pam would call me the afternoon after I preached, and would say, "Denice, that was powerful today. You spoke with such authority and passion. You helped me today."

That always meant so much to me because sometimes you're not sure of yourself. Also, when we were young, Pam tried to "polish" me. I was one of her favorite speakers. Isn't that funny? I would hear her laughing in the audience at the things I said.

With the help of God, the church drew people who were searching for answers. All people are the same; they need God. We attracted doctors, lawyers, teachers, and ditch diggers—all backgrounds. It was beautiful.

Our church, with black and white sitting together, side by side, not caring who they were or what they did in life. It was beautiful seeing an elegantly dressed woman sitting next to an ex-prostitute, and doctors, and lawyers sitting next to ex-drug addicts. Nobody cared.

They were there as brothers and sisters in the Lord, all wanting to be fed the Word of God. All treated equally.

We had stable marriages in our congregation, and strong marriages were the foundation of the church. Women together hold most churches, but not at Christian Life Church. Steve led the men.

We went after marriages and taught what the Word says about a woman and a man. We were young, and this helped draw in young couples and college students. Steve and I had our talk show that aired on TV, Monday through Friday. It was called Heart to Heart. The men in the church were always asking when I was going to speak, which I was a high compliment. I told jokes and made people laugh as I walloped them hard with the truth, and they never saw it coming.

Steve had a powerful ability to teach with authority, the authority God had given him in his calling. He spoke with excellence, and you could feel his heartbeat as the words came forth with passion. Please know that I say all this to show you how God can take two people that are a broken mess, turn their life around, and make their lives matter. I boast of God. Without Him, Steve, and I would be nothing.

I HAVE LEARNED:

Seek the Father as hard as the Father is seeking you.

SHARE

27

You're Pregnant, Again!

WHEN I GAVE birth to our son, Stephen, the first thing I said to my son was, "There you are, and I've been looking for you for a long time."

Steve went to the waiting room to announce the birth of his son. What did Steve do? He flexed his muscles for everyone. He's the man.

We were sure we were through having children, and I had a history of female problems, so a few weeks after I recovered from childbirth, I went into the hospital to have a hysterectomy. We felt it was the best decision. I checked into the hospital the night before for early morning surgery. Just as I was falling asleep, the nurse came into the room, "Denice, your doctor wants you to call him at home."

I called the doctor, "Denice, you have to go home. You're pregnant."

"Doctor, I can't be. There is no way."

He laughed, "There is away, and you are."

I remembered Steve, and I had gone to be on a television show, The P. T. L. Club. Our son, Stephen, was three weeks old. I convinced Steve it was safe to have sex because I had not yet had a regular cycle.

While we were there doing the show, we had dinner with Dale Evans, one of my childhood heroes. Roy Rogers had already gone to be with the Lord. I told her that she, and Roy, along with Roy's horse Trigger, were in my life every day when I was a child, and I had wanted to be a cowgirl, just like her. I remember whispering to Steve at the table, sitting across from Dale Evans, "Can you believe this?" Under my breath, I whispered, "Destiny."

Anyway, back to trying to explain how I got pregnant. I told my doctor I would not go home until he proved it to me. The nurse took me downstairs to do an ultrasound.

I asked her, "Do you see a baby on that screen?"

She answered, "I'm not allowed to say."

Plastic Tulips in the Winter

"Listen, I just gave birth to a baby, shake your head yes or no. Now I'm going to ask you again. Do you see a baby on that screen?" She nodded her head in affirmation, yes.

I called Steve at the church office, and when he heard me say his name in a stretched out, desperate way, he started laughing. "You're pregnant."

Later that day, as I held our newborn baby boy in my arms, Steve, and I explained to Stacy, who was thirteen years old, and Misty, eight years old, that I didn't have surgery, because we had a surprise for them. "Momma and Daddy are going to have another baby."

Stacy was so embarrassed that we were pregnant again. "Would y'all please just stop it?!" As she walked out of the room. We both laughed.

Nine Months later, a few hours before I went into labor with our fourth child, I heard the voice of God prompting me, *"When the enemy makes a threat, it is only a threat if you do not listen, but if you listen, it will turn into reality."* I woke up, wrote it down on a piece of paper, thinking I was to preach on that sometime in the future. What I didn't know was that I would be the one needing those words over the next several hours. My labor began, and on the way to the hospital, I told Steve what God had spoken to me.

"Denice, let's go have a baby, and we'll talk about that later."

"I just want you to remember. We are to preach that." Then I leaned forward in pain.

During the delivery, I noticed my doctor's look of concern. My baby stuck in the birth canal. The heart had stopped; the baby was not breathing. The doctor began to make the adjustments to pull it out, as it was too late to do a C-section. The baby was too far down the birth canal, and when I saw the look on his face, I knew I was in trouble.

I asked, "Steve, is everything all right?"

"Everything is all right," he answered firmly.

Again, I asked, "Steve, is everything all right?"

"Denice, everything is all right." He responded.

The doctor listened to Steve and me as we talked back and forth. There was no way the baby, without a heartbeat, and oxygen was going to be born alive. It seemed like it was taking forever to get the lifeless baby out of my body.

One of the nurses began pushing my stomach as the doctor instructed her until the baby finally appeared.

Plastic Tulips in the Winter

The doctor held up my lifeless girl. On her back, arms and legs dangling. She looked like a perfect baby doll, except for the color, a dark blue-grey. I asked Steve again, "Steve, is everything all right?"

He answered, "Everything is all right."

We stayed in agreement that everything was all right.

I looked at the doctor; he had a concerned look.

Again, I looked at Steve and asked, "Steve, is everything all right?"

Steve responded, "Denice, everything is all right."

We continued to say that to each other. As the doctor was holding our lifeless baby girl, I remembered what God had said to me right before my labor started. "When the enemy makes a threat, it is only a threat if you do not listen, but if you listen, it will turn into reality."

Suddenly, our baby girl gave out a cry. Steve took her in his hands, held her up toward heaven, and declared, "Her name is Denice."

The Word God had spoken to me now made sense; this had been a "threat." Denice Lynne Vickers, May 23, 1984. She looked like a china doll with a head full of black hair. She and Stephen were ten months apart.

It was like having twins— two in diapers, and with bottles. The joy I had was so enormous. I wasn't sure I could fit it all into my heart.

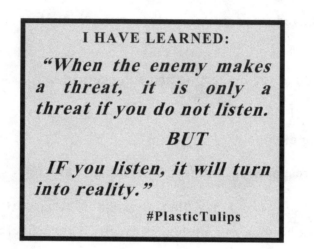

I HAVE LEARNED:

"When the enemy makes a threat, it is only a threat if you do not listen.

BUT

IF you listen, it will turn into reality."

#PlasticTulips

28

Life's Fast Track

WE MOVED INTO a brand new home. We found out Governor George Wallace lived across the street from us with a guard gate at the entrance of the driveway. We knew he used a wheelchair and needed his privacy, but that did not deter my Misty. She was nine years old and had my personality. She got to know the guard at the gate, and he got a kick out of her.

It was Halloween, and Stacy and Misty wanted to trick or treat at Governor Wallace's house, so the guard escorted them in after receiving permission from the Governor, who was glad to meet them.

Governor Wallace said, "I'm sorry, but I have no candy to give you." He told the guard, "Go get me two pictures, and I will sign them for these two young ladies."

Misty came home disappointed, "All he gave me was this dumb picture with his name on it. I wanted candy." We laughed at her because she didn't understand who he was.

It was a beautiful neighborhood. Our neighbors were successful, fun-loving, cheerful, and colorful. One character, on Christmas Day, cruised the community on a motorized toilet with his trumpet in hand, announcing to all that Christmas was here. Funny huh?

I wrote my first book, "God, Let Me Out of This Marriage," and began to speak on all the Christian television shows around the country. I struggled, wanting to stay home with my children, so I let the book do the talking for me.

Our home life consisted of homework, school projects, braces, school plays, cheerleading, and barbecues around our pool. In the winter, we took the children on snow skiing trips with aunts, uncles, and cousins to Steamboat, Colorado. Steve bought a ski boat so that we could spend Saturdays on the lake with our children. They loved to water ski, and Stacy and Misty brought their boyfriends along. Life was good. Our two youngest children Stephen, and Denice, loved doing everything the older sisters did, and they were growing like weeds.

Plastic Tulips in the Winter

During that time, I was diagnosed with rheumatoid arthritis and dealt with a lot of pain. We hired a full-time maid to help me with the house and my two youngest children. They loved her, and always greeted her with a big kiss on the lips.

Our church had as many blacks as whites. You must understand, at the time, that was not normal in the South. We were the first fully integrated church in the state of Alabama. It wasn't unusual for the local news to show up at our service with their cameras. They would interview us and ask how we accomplished such a beautiful yet difficult thing in the city that was the heart of the Civil Rights Movement. We would tell them it was only because of God. But we did make a lot of white churches mad. Some pastors believed they helped the blacks by giving mission money to keep them on the right side of town.

One night, I sat Denice and Stephen on the kitchen counter. They were about five years old. "Now, kids, this weekend, Daddy, and I are going to take you to meet Daddy's aunt that you have never met."

Denice looked at me and asked, "Is she black or white?" Steve and I had a good laugh, realizing, here we were in the Deep South, and our daughter wasn't sure what color our kinfolk were. Our children were not raised to be prejudiced.

My daughters, Stacy, Misty, and Denice were cheerleaders, and Misty voted homecoming queen. Their brother, Stephen, was a singer in a band, and a stage actor. I know that this sounds like a mother bragging, but I believed my children were so beautiful that they could stop traffic.

We raised our children in a beautiful home with a swimming pool, trampoline, and a playhouse in the back yard. It was a lot different from my childhood.

Over the years, we started buying rental property. Momma moved into one of them.

I sewed making bedspreads, and drapes for our girls' rooms, and always had a craft project like making lamps, and collecting antique teapots, and bells. Then there was still this feeling there was a treasure to be found. I would have dreams about a treasure and a waterfall. But as of the writing of this book, I have not found one yet. But I will still enjoy the hope of finding one. I am a treasure hunter.

Steve earned his doctorate and got his pilot's license—two of his goals. He bought a jet plane as he continued to Pastor, using the jet get to churches all over the country. It was part of our mission.

Plastic Tulips in the Winter

When pastors needed a pastor for themselves, they called Steve. He could get to them in their time of need. No pastor was unimportant to Steve. It didn't matter how small or how large the congregation was. They knew he cared about them. Pastors go through the same trials and tribulations that their flocks go through, but it is hard for them to turn to someone for help.

I saw the world with Steve. God allowed us to go to places I would have never dreamed. We flew to Atlanta, Georgia, and a Limo picked us up to attend the grand opening of the new office of the Cochran firm. We celebrated at the home of "Home Run King," Hank Aaron. Stevie Wonder was performing in the back yard. God opens amazing doors that no man can close.

We traveled in ministry to Bangkok, Koh Samui, and Chiang Mai, Thailand; Switzerland, Germany; Monaco, France; the Philippines; Rangoon, Burma; Kathmandu, Nepal; Mexico, St Thomas, Puerto Rico, the Dominican Republic, and Kenya. In Uganda, we put in a well for over five hundred families. We helped feed starving children in these countries. We preached to the pastors so that they could give good spiritual food to the people. We built churches, orphanages, Bible schools in different nations. We began a ministry for African pastors who were crying out for help and instruction.

Once when we were in Katmandu, Nepal, Steve got a driver to take us around to see the city. The driver stopped at the top of a mountain for us to have a look. I was so excited. I opened the door to step out, not realizing he had stopped on the edge of a cliff, and when I took my first step out of the car, I began to fall down the cliff in mid-air. I could hear myself screaming out, "Jesus!" as I fell through the air, breaking tree limbs that bounced me around for what seemed like forever. I finally landed face down in a huge mud hole, which turned out to be a pig's pen. Covered from head to toe with blood, pig poop, and mud, I jumped up, threw my hands in the air, and yelled out, "I'm alive!"

Steve and the driver were looking down from the top of that mountain, horrified.

I was glad to be alive and no broken bones. It provided us many laughs over the years. Steve always said, "Denice, living with you is an adventure in itself."

While I was in Jinja, Uganda, I was sitting on the porch of a small cottage by the Nile River, drinking a cup of coffee. I watched monkeys swinging from fruit trees in the yard. I was thinking about how amazing my life was. How a little girl from Alabama, who could whoop any boy's tail, and stuck frogs in her pocket, could end up in Africa. I thought about how my life could have taken a different course if it were not for God. Everything good in my life is because of Him. Without Him, I would not have made it.

To think about the fact, He spoke to that fourteen-year-old girl as she was sweeping the carpet. My gosh, if I had not believed that He could talk to his children, what a beautiful life I would have missed. I'm not saying there haven't been times of sadness, tests, and trials. Trust me when I say, we had times where it was raining on us, nights that were so long, and dark, but we looked to God to get through the storms of life. He's been there all along the way. We knew we were blessed as we ran after God and obeyed Him. Sometimes I just felt He spoiled me. I guess He wanted me to feel that way. Obeying God and doing His will energized our life. I boast of God's blessings. Without him, I would not have had this life. Life is Beautiful. With the good, the bad, and the ugly, God is still God.

Those were the thoughts that ran through my mind as I heard the voice of God say to me, "Go get a pen and paper."

I wrote the first page of this book and stopped at the place where I asked, "Momma, are we there yet?" It flowed out, without even thinking of what I was writing down. I knew I had just started a book. [Now, look at you; you're reading my book, "Smile."]

Steve and I recording our daily TV show.

ONLY IN AMERICA

I have never been able to find a place where I couldn't embarrass myself, and this place was now on my list. If something crazy is going to happen, it's going to happen to me. That summer on our vacation Steve, and I took our kids to Disney World in Orlando Fl.

There is a building you can enter to see a short film about how Walt Disney came up with Disney World. We thought that would be interesting.

The crowd pushed their way into the darkroom. We stood in front of the screen. Somehow, we got separated from each other without me realizing it.

I love cuddling; it was dark, and I placed my arm around Steve. We were hip-to-hip and cheek-to-cheek. I also like to shock Steve when he is not expecting anything. So, I'll just say I got fresh in the dark with him. The lights turned on, and I turned my face toward Steve, whom I had snuggled up during the show. I was shocked. It wasn't Steve. Instead, staring at me with a big smile on his face was an Asian man.

Gasping for breath, I stuttered, "I . . . I thought you were my husband." He smiled, and in his broken English, "It's okay."

I left the building and found Steve and the kids. "Do you know what I was doing in the dark just now?" I excitedly tried to express my discomfort, "I was in the dark hugging on another man, getting fresh with him."

Steve laughed at me, "Why didn't you check to make sure it was me?"

"Steve, you walked in with me. How could you leave me like that?" He just laughed and shook his head.

Misty spoke up, "I saw you, Momma."

"Misty, why didn't you tell me I was hugging on that man?" She said, "I thought you knew."

Somewhere in this world, there is a short Japanese man who tells all his friends, "Go to America. The women there will surprise you in the dark, and you will love it."

HOLIDAYS, AND FAMILY

My sisters, brother, and Mom continued to be my closest friends. We attended church, went to movies, and dinners together. We shared our Easters, Thanksgivings, and Christmases as a family.

I always said our home was loud with love & laughter!

Plastic Tulips in the Winter

During football season, every weekend, Steve, and our son-in-law would be cheering from the living room while I made chili, and of course, fudge while my daughters and daughter-in-law laughed around the kitchen table. Holidays we spent dancing and grilling around our pool or by the fire. Music, fun, and laughter were always abundant.

Thanksgivings were at Janice's house, and Christmas Eve was at Pam's. Christmas day, we stayed home. I always cooked a big meal ahead of time to serve mid-afternoon.

On Christmas Eve, Momma gets showered with gifts from all her children, and grandchildren. She went on everybody's family vacation. We put ski boots on her in the snow in Steamboat, Colorado, and pulled her around on a flat surface. We always spoiled Momma. She was our queen, and the grandchildren called her Granny and Duchess.

Janice married her dream man, Colonel Tom Willard, and had a formal military wedding. He worked at the Pentagon in Washington, DC.

It was funny—the once-hippie was now a Colonel's wife. They lived in Boston, and Tom was commander over the building of military satellites. They bought an old Southern antebellum home for Mom to live in, in

Alabama. Janice and Tom filled it with antique furniture they had collected, and they opened a store for Mom to manage. It was called "The Holiday House."

Mom rented out some of the bedrooms to single, young men in the church. She loved mothering them and speaking into their lives.

It wasn't long before Janice and Tom retired to be with all the family. Between the two of them, they had six sons, Mike, Raymond, Chris, Ben, Mike, and John. They took Momma on overseas trips to Korea, Germany, and Hawaii. Momma was becoming a world traveler. Isn't that funny?

Over the years, many people have told me that Janice had been the one that led them to the Lord.

####

Pam and her husband had two sons and three daughters. Their children kept them busy with sports, cheerleading, and all that goes with raising children. Pam loved being a mother and was always reading books on parenting.

One day, Pam stopped by my house, "I believe I have found my calling." I looked at her as I listened.

Plastic Tulips in the Winter

She continued, "I'm an intercessor. I will spend time praying for people. That's what I can do."

I smiled, "Well, that's great, Pam." I knew Pam was always praying for people and encouraging the young women in our church. At the time, I didn't know where all this would lead her. Pam was so neat in every way. If there was the slightest odor in the room, Pam was the one to notice it. Blood and vomit were two words you would not use in the same sentence when in her presence. That would change.

Pam drove her expensive car back and forth to Birmingham, Alabama, which was over an hour's drive, taking women for their cancer treatment. Pam provided them with a bucket to throw up in while she prayed for them all the way there and back.

A guy named Mark visited our church and answered the altar call for prayer. Pam met him for the first time at the altar. Pam was a prayer partner, praying for people who came to the altar. Mark was a drag queen.

Now, when I say, "drag queen," I mean a flamboyant drag queen with hands going, hips moving, body swaging, head swaying, girl talking, hair flipping, and dressed in women's clothes from head to toe. Well, it was just plum confusing. Mark had some real disadvantages as a drag queen—he was white, tall, about six-four, and way too skinny. It just did not work for him at all.

Mark's family had disowned him years ago, and even gay people didn't like him. They said he was too flamboyant, and he got on their nerves. Mark had nobody, but Pam had compassion for him and became his friend. He called her often for prayer.

One day, he came to her and told her he was dying of Aids. She led him to the Lord and prayed with him. Mark truly got born again.

During Mark's last days in the hospital, his only friend, Pam, the intercessor, stayed with him until he took his last breath. No one was there to see him leave this world, but Pam.

Pam stopped by my house the day Mark passed away. With her perfectly folded Kleenex in her hand, she wiped away her tears, "Denice, Mark, and I held hands and sang "Jesus Loves Me" as tears ran down his face. He took his last breath still singing, for the Bible tells me so."

Pam stood in my kitchen and cried over Mark. I looked at my sister at that moment and thought about what a beautiful soul she had. She loved what the world would have said was unlovable.

Plastic Tulips in the Winter

####

Leeann and Kenny had a daughter named Logan. Leeann had a dream of owning her own business. She began to decorate all the wealthy homes in town for Christmas. It became a hot ticket in the city to have Leeann decorate your home for the holidays. She then opened her designer home store.

It was a beautiful Tuscan structure with a hair salon, spa, boutique, and furniture showroom. Leeann became successful in decorating houses, vacation homes, and redesigning office and apartment buildings. It was a God-given gift, and she loved every minute of it.

LEFT TO RIGHT

Janice, Leeann, Mom, Charlie, Pam, and me. Photo was taken at the wedding of my oldest daughter, Stacy.

29

Tell Us, You Found Nothing

MOMMA WAS diagnosed with cancer of the liver. We transferred her to a cancer hospital at Keesler A.F.B. in Biloxi, Mississippi, to have a new test done. The test came back with the same report. She only had a few weeks to live.

The doctors decided they would open her up to do a biopsy. The night before surgery, around midnight, Janice, Pam, Charlie, and I were at a restaurant. We agreed that God is a big God, and He has the last say in this matter. I told them we needed to go up to the hospital where Momma was and request the film of cancer that was on her liver. "We need to look at our enemy and command it to leave."

I had learned the power of hope in God. Hope is the rope you swing on to get to faith. Faith releases God's promises. If you do not have hope, you will never have faith.

The night nurse told us it was illegal for her to show them to us. I looked at her desperate, "Now, you listen to me. Our mother is dying. We believe in the power of laying on of hands and getting into the power of agreement. You are not going to deny Momma's kids from doing that, are you?" She pushed away from her desk, "Follow me."

The nurse took us to a room were files kept. She held the film for us to look at. It looked like a massive cluster of grapes on her liver. We stared in silence, looking at the enemy that dared take Momma's life. We laid our hands on the film and commanded cancer to get out of our mother's body, in the name of Jesus.

The next morning, before they took Momma to surgery, we began to dance around her bed, singing, *"Satan, the blood of Jesus is against you."*

Momma laughed as we were doing all the dances of our youth to that song. We stopped dancing and singing when the doctor walked in. I asked, "Doctor, Momma has always had a weak bladder. I was wondering, while you have her open, will you put a few tacks in her bladder, so when she laughs, she won't pee on herself?"

Plastic Tulips in the Winter

He moved his head back with his chin down with amazement that I could ask such a foolish thing. He paused to gather his words. "We do not do corrective surgery at a time like this."

I responded, "Oh, I get it, but can you just promise me that if you open Momma up, and the cancer is not there, you will tack up her bladder?" He looked at me, "Sure, I can promise you that."

After five hours of surgery, the doctor walked out, scratching his head. He stood talking to another doctor. I grabbed him by the hand and pulled him in front of Janice, Pam, and Charlie, as we all began to jump up and down, screaming with joy. I yelled, "Tell us you found nothing!"

He looked up at the ceiling, paused, and then looked at us and spoke in a very somber manner, "I found nothing."

I asked, "Did you tack her bladder?"

"I tacked her bladder," he responded.

We were shouting and jumping up and down like children in a candy store.

The waiting room packed with people with their loved ones in surgery. They heard what was being said and began to line up for their miracle. No one spoke about forming a line if you want prayer, but everyone just got in line. God took it out of her body during the night before surgery. Momma got a miracle.

As Momma being rolled out of recovery. I walked along beside her, "Momma, you got a miracle — the cancer is gone."

Mom responded with her declaration, "God is a good God." We began to sing to her:

God is a good God,

God don't ever change,

God is a Good God,

that's why I'll ever Praise His name

I'm a telling you, God is a good God

The doctor asked us, "What did you do to make it disappear?" We answered him, "We believed God."

I am telling you the reader to understand no matter what you face in life, remember this, "BUT GOD."

The night nurse had left for her vacation, but the next morning, she called up the hospital to find out the results of the surgery. When she was told it wasn't there, she called her grandmother to tell her all about it. Her grandmother had always told her about these things happening, but she had never witnessed it for herself. She said it was life-changing for her. About 20 years passed, and no cancer — a miracle.

Life was like we were on a fast train, looking out the window, seeing it speed by. A lot of living was going on. I always reminded my children that family is the strongest army on earth, and don't forget it.

People come and go through your life, but there is nothing stronger than blood. You accept each other's imperfections, and you do it for life. No matter what, always believing the best will happen to them. I realize I have become my mother, still making declarations to my children. There is power in our words, for good or bad.

I HAVE LEARNED:

HOPE in GOD is the rope you swing on to get to FAITH.

FAITH gets you to His promises.

If you do not have HOPE, you will never have FAITH.

CHOOSE TO HOPE AGAIN!

#PlasticTulips

30
A Glass Of Wine

MOMMA WAS NOW on blood pressure pills due to high blood pressure. The doctor told her to drink a glass of red wine every evening. He said it would help keep her blood pressure down. Leeann got her a gallon jug of cheap wine, and Momma put it on top of her refrigerator. I told her she should drink it, but every time I walked into her house, I looked at that bottle to check the wine level. Momma was not drinking it. I asked her why she didn't know.

One afternoon, I was hurrying to meet Pam and Momma at a baby shower for a young girl in our church. The phone rang, and Steve answered it. He talked for a few seconds and then hung up. "Denice, the drug store just called. Your Mom is there and has fallen."

We jumped into the car and drove as fast as we could. It was only a few blocks from our home. We drove up and saw a fire truck and an ambulance. "My God," I yelled.

Running in, I saw paramedics around her, trying to get her to speak. "Mrs. Burge, we are going to take you in the ambulance."

In a slow, slurred tone, "No, you're not."

I spoke up. "Momma, yes, they are."

Her body appeared paralyzed. One side of her face was different, and I knew the signs looked like a stroke. While we followed the ambulance to the hospital, I took out my cell phone and called my brother and sisters. We had no idea how bad she was. Paralyzed and over the next two months, she couldn't speak or move.

Momma had been strong-minded and independent after God got hold of all our lives. She was the glue in our family. We couldn't bear to see her in this state. She had movement on one side of her body as she lay in the hospital, but she was not able to communicate. We were devastated.

Momma was never left alone. She was taken to another floor to begin rehabilitation. If she didn't show signs that she could do certain things, she would be sent home, and would not improve. They moved her from the wheelchair to a workout mat. They then sat her down to see if she could sit alone. She began to slump over, lying helplessly on her side. I sat down beside her and whispered in her ear, "Momma, please try with everything in you." I cried.

A nurse at the rehab center told me, "I have worked in other states at other rehabilitation hospitals, but I have never seen so many stroke victims like you see in the South."

I asked her, "Is it because of our fried food, high fat diet?"

She said it was because of the Bible belt. "You know most Southern Christians think it's a sin to have a glass of wine." She didn't know she was talking to a preacher's wife.

The Bible talks about not drinking to excess and drunkenness. I always told Steve I thought it looked romantic seeing a man and woman at a restaurant having a glass of wine together.

The doctors were talking about the health benefits of red wine, so I began to do my research on the matter, spiritually and medically.

I knew preachers who drank in the South but only in the privacy of their homes, as not to offend other

Christians. I also knew preachers in the Northern states who thought Southern preachers took the scriptures to the extreme by saying it's a sin. I was going to be open for God to show me if it was going to separate me from Him.

Steve grew up in a home that had wine at the dinner table. We had preached in other countries where the preachers drank alcohol but thought caffeine was a sin. Steve and I loved our cup of coffee every morning.

My journey began, and I started having a glass of wine with my evening meal. At first, I felt I was sinning. I had to ask myself, is this conviction of the Holy Spirit, or is it guilt from the way I was raised? I realized it was my upbringing. I know this: The Bible says if you drink to excess, it makes you act like a fool, just like how overeating is harmful to your health. Obesity will kill you, but we do not quit eating.

I have seen severely overweight Christians judge people for drinking. Isn't it funny when you think about a three-hundred-pound Christian sitting there, eating a bowl of ice cream piled on top of a piece of cake, judging a person for drinking a glass of wine? Funny, huh?

But I must tell you we have lost a loved one to alcohol addiction.

Plastic Tulips in the Winter

A beautiful soul died early before his time. Therefore, I don't take lightly this warning I give you: Any addiction is dangerous. Whether it is an addiction to food, cigarettes, alcohol, etc., addictions can shorten your life. Some people come from a home of addiction, which can be genetically set for that addiction. Yes, God can and will help you break that in your family but not without you helping yourself.

The Bible says, Strong drink will make you act like a fool, but it does not mean not to drink. Just a warning. But I decided to put this in my story because it was my journey.

Now, I was telling you about us at the hospital. Janice, Pam, and I stood around Momma in the hospital room. She was staring straight at the ceiling, not even blinking. Her breathing was slow to the point that we couldn't tell if she was breathing.

Pam said, "I want to be the one to get Momma's last breath. I want to be there when she takes it so she can breathe into me her anointing." We worshiped our mother.

Momma had been a kind, loving, and beautiful person. She was a mother who loved her children with every breath she took. We all wanted to be like her.

Janice laughed, "What gives you the right to get her last breath." The two of them were having this conversation and looking down at Mom.

I spoke up, "Neither one of you are going to get her last breath. I will be the one, so you two might as well stop arguing over it."

Janice, being the character that she is, leaned down into Momma's face, "Is anybody in there?"

Pam pulled Janice away from Momma's face. "Janice quit it."

Janice again, "Is anybody in there?" In a loud voice, and as clear as words can be spoken, Momma answered, "You girls quit it."

Janice responded in a voice like that from The Exorcist movie, "She's back," we laughed.

Momma would never totally recover. She spent the next six years in a wheelchair with only the use of one arm, and in a diaper. She could speak, but she was helpless and frail from then on.

She moved in with Charlie, and his boyfriend, Jimmy, who became her caregivers. Momma loved Jimmy and treated him like a son. He couldn't have treated her any better if she had been his mother. Charlie played her Christian worship music while she ate her breakfast and let her watch her Christian TV channels all day long. Jimmy took Momma in her wheelchair to a little Methodist church nearby on Sundays.

I asked Mom several times over the next six years, "How do you deal with being in a wheelchair?" She lifted one arm into the air and declared, "I trust God."

I asked, "Do you ever get depressed about it?"

"Yes, but then I just turn my trust toward Him."

I asked, "Momma, do you really believe it is wrong to drink alcohol?" "No," she answered.

"Then why did you teach us it was a sin?"

"Because my Momma told me it was a sin,"

I heard a story once. A mother was teaching her daughter how to cook a ham in the oven, the Southern way. She showed her daughter that you take the whole ham, set it on the cutting board, and chop both ends of the ham off before you put it in your pot to stick in the oven. The daughter asked, "Why do you cut the ends off?"

"I don't know. That's the way my momma taught me how to cook a ham."

Suzy said, "Let's call grandmother and ask her why."

Suzy's momma called her mother, "I'm teaching Suzy how to cook a ham in the oven, and we have a question. Why did you always cut both ends off the ham before you cooked it?"

She laughed, "Because my pot was too small."

Traditions are passed down from generation to generation until someone begins asking questions, even in the church. Some preachers are afraid to search for the truth, for it could cost them in their community. I say, "Let's give them something to talk about."

31

Nellie's Spa & Aromatherapy

Summer 2004

IT WAS HOT, humid in Alabama. Charlie brought Momma to stay with me for ten days while he and Jimmy went on a cruise. They desperately needed a break, and it was a well-deserved one since they had been taking care of Momma. I wanted to see if I could take care of her. Lifting her from her wheelchair was going to be challenging, as I was dealing with my own from rheumatoid arthritis.

I had it all planned out. While Steve was in Africa for two weeks, I was going to give her my full attention. It was going to be Nellie's ten days at the spa.

Since my master bedroom was downstairs and knowing there was no way I could get Momma upstairs to one of the guest bedrooms, I ordered a blow-up Aero Bed mattress, which I put on the floor in my bedroom.

If she needed me during the night, I would be right there.

Several days before, I had gone to Hobby Lobby and bought a beautiful brown wicker basket and two bleached pine eight by ten photo frames. I filled the basket with Bath & Body Works products, Moonlight Path Bubble Bath, True Blue Spa soap, a butter creamy cleansing bar, Aromatherapy Spearmint Massage oil, sugar scrub, and Cherry Blossom Moisturizing Cream. Each item tied with a tiny satin ribbon bow in pale colors of pink, blue, lavender, and green and then wrapped in soft netting. A bottle of Michael Kors Island perfume, and two new face towels in mint green, and lavender were rolled up and added. Beside the basket, placed on my garden tub, were two photo frames. In the frames, a note was written:

NELLIE'S

Spa & Aromatherapy

Enjoy Deep Sleep

Bubble Bath

Therapeutic Massages

Manicure & Pedicure

& Facials

All this is for you.

Relax, play & laugh

with your
grandchildren.

Your attendants are
your

loving children.

Know you are loved.

Denice

Dear Momma,

You are loved and adored. For the next

ten days, I will bless you for all you have done for me in my heart and my life. Every morning you will receive a full:

NELLIE'S SPA TREATMENT

I will cook your favorite foods. We will watch your favorite movies together, Titanic, Gone with The Wind, and of course, your boyfriend, Mel Gibson's, Man, Without A Face, are waiting for you. We will have a wonderful ten days together. You will be reminded how much your children love you. No one has touched my life like you, and now it is my time to be a blessing in your life. I love you, Momma, With all my heart.

Denice

Plastic Tulips in the Winter

Charlie pulled into the circle driveway in front of my house. I ran out to greet them and opened the backseat car door, dancing and saying, "Where's my baby? Where's the Duchess?"

Lifting her only good arm, she gave a queen's wave, and the look on her face said it all. Her skin was soft, like a baby's. Her rosy, high cheekbones showed with a smile that lit up the world. She giggled, "Hey, Baby."

Charlie opened the trunk of the car, pulled out the wheelchair, snapped the footrest back on, and threw the extra gel seat cushion into the chair. I was busy kissing Momma all over her face as if she were a baby while she laughed, "Oh, my girl."

I danced around and sang, "Party, party, we're going to party."

Momma lifted that one arm, and made her declaration, "Yes, we are, God, is good!"

Charlie was trying to get me to move out of the way. He needed to lift her out of the car and place her in the wheelchair. Jimmy pulled the luggage out of the back seat.

"Y'all come on in. Let's get my baby inside so I can love on her."

Charlie wheeled Momma into the living room and began to explain her medications to me. He was very organized, and he had written instructions on how to dispense her medicine, how many to give her, and what to give her in case she was in pain.

"Charlie, I've got this. Don't worry. We will be fine. We're going to have our vacation while you and Jimmy are on yours."

Charlie looked at me, "I'm not going to think about anything but myself."

"Good, go have fun. Don't think of us at all."

They left for their cruise, and I was ready and willing to give Momma the works. We ate a snack, and then it was time to put her to bed. I gave her the medicines for the evening and pulled the potty-chair upside the wheelchair. "I'm going to stand you up, and you lean toward me."

"Denice, are you sure you can do this?" She questioned.

I assured her that together, we could do this, but her fear of falling made me scared. I moved her footrest back from the wheelchair and placed her feet firmly on the floor. In a calm, loving voice, "Momma, put your good arm around my neck."

Plastic Tulips in the Winter

I began to lift her, and pain shot up from my arthritic hands and spine. Momma tensed up, and screamed out in pain, scaring us both. "You're killing me! God, help me," she screamed.

"Momma try not to tense up. You're stiffening your legs, and I don't want to drop you."

I felt helpless, but bless her heart, she was helpless. I couldn't let her fall. I had to take all the weight because she was unable to help. I twisted her dead weight over to the potty chair and tried to pull down her navy-blue sweatpants, and diaper at the same time.

"Thank you, Lord," she shouted out and gave her Queens wave to God. The sweat was pouring from my armpits as my heavy breathing calmed down.

"Thank you, Lord," giving my own shout out.

She responded with a gasp, "Yes, thank you, Lord."

"Momma, sit on the potty, and do your business while I undress you." Suddenly she broke out into a song smiling as she sang her favorite song by Rod Stewart, "Have I told you lately that I love you."

After I put her in a large man's t-shirt, I realized I was going to have to go through that ordeal to get her back into the wheelchair, and then from the wheelchair to the Aero bed. I finally got Momma into bed and placed extra washrags in her diaper to help absorb the urine. I put on her white support stockings, and her night leg braces gave her pills and slid her neck pillow under her neck. I kissed her face, "Now go to sleep, Creep."

She laughed as I pulled the top sheet up under her chin as I teased her. She loved it when I called her "Creep."

I began to pray over her, "God, thank you for blessing me with Momma. Give her good sleep tonight. Help her not to have pain so that she will wake up rested in the morning, Amen."

She took over the prayer and prayed that Charlie and Jimmy would have a good time on their cruise, overall her children, grandchildren, and great-grandchildren. There were forty-five people she prayed for, and that included Jimmy, and Charlie's dogs, the boxers, Wes, and Frankie. She finished with, "God, bless my Denice for taking care of me. Amen."

I woke the next morning to the thought; I didn't hear a sound out of mom all night. I found the aero bed had deflated. Her body was flat on the floor. The sheet covered her face. And the air in the mattress had formed a taco around her. I leaped from my bed, panicked, and thought, oh no, I killed Momma. Pulling the sheet back from her face, I shouted, "Momma, are you, all right?"

Her eyes opened wide, "I slept wonderfully." Her rosy cheeks and smile lit up my heart.

"Momma, your mattress deflated."

She laughed. My mind was racing about how I was going to lift the dead weight off the floor. I put my arms under her arms and lifted her into the wheelchair.

"I'm going to start a bubble bath, and then we will get you into the tub."

She loved laying in a hot tub for as long as you would let her. Throwing her right arm up in the air with a smile as big as the world, "Yes, yes, yes, Amen, Yea."

I started the tub and then returned to wheel her into the bathroom only to find that the wheelchair would not fit through the bathroom door. I thought, "You got to be kidding, not this."

However, "Don't worry, Momma, I have another plan." I assured her I could handle anything. She waited until I returned from the storage room with a desk chair. It had a black leather seat and back with no armrest. I shifted her body from the wheelchair over to the office chair. Then rolling it beside the tub filled with bubbles.

She relaxed in her bath as I sat on the side of the tub to visit while she soaked in her bubbles. I began to show her all her beauty products in the basket I had made up for her. I read to her what the two picture frames said.

Mom made her declaration, giving a wave to God, smiling while enjoying all the pampering, "I am blessed. Yes, I am blessed."

"Momma, your skin is dry. Let's add oil to the water."

"Denice, you are so good to me. All my children are. I am so blessed. Yes, I'm blessed, I'm blessed, amen," she declared.

I poured the oil into the bathtub, and said to her, "You deserve to be blessed. You are a wonderful Momma." She raised her hand in the air, and added, "I love my children with every breath that is within me."

I smiled at her. "All right, you little brat. I'm going to go to start breakfast. You lie here and relax."

She laughed at me for calling her a brat. "You're such a crazy girl, Denice."

Plastic Tulips in the Winter

I returned, telling her it was time to get out. "Let's drain the tub so that I can stand in it to lift you out." I began to lift her and realized she was slippery from the oil. I knew I would not be able to do this on my own. I called Janice, "Janice, I have a problem."

Janice asked in a tone like, I told you so, "What have you done to Momma?"

I dreaded telling her, "I put oil in her bathwater, and now she is too slippery for me to get her out of the tub."

"I told you this was going to be too hard for you."

Firmly, "Janice, let's don't go there." I already had a bad start.

"Don't move her. I will be there in a few minutes." Janice and I could get her out.

Every night for the next few nights, I cried myself to sleep, soaking the pillow with my silent tears. I was mad that taking care of her was so hard. I was angry that my body hurt, and I felt sorry for myself. I was not physically able to do this. It was much harder than taking care of a baby. She would feel she needed to get on her potty chair, and then after all the maneuvering, find out she didn't need to go. This would occur every few minutes. Finally, she would end up going in her diaper. I'm telling you, that was a story in itself.

I wanted this to work so that she could stay with me more often. She thanked me continually; bless her heart, she was so grateful. The pain in my own body fought me every move I made.

By the time Charlie and Jimmy arrived from their trip. I was glad that day had come. I was going to miss her, but my body was in pain, and I needed to crash and recover. Jimmy spent the night with his parents, and Charlie slept upstairs in one of my guest rooms. My kids were older now and had their own places.

32

Jerk This Car In Reverse

T HE NEXT MORNING, she was still sleeping when I went outside and found Charlie sitting by the pool having a cup of coffee and smoking a cigarette. I poured myself a cup of coffee and joined him. I told him all that had occurred while he was gone, we drank our coffee and laughed as I told him all about it. "Charlie, I don't see how you do it."

He looked at me, "Sometimes I go out in the backyard and throw a fit and cry by myself, but I know I'm doing the right thing. I will not regret taking care of Mom."

I smiled at him, "If it ever gets to be too much, just let us know. We'll put mom in a nursing home and visit her every day."

"I can't do that."

Changing the subject, "Charlie, I woke up with a thought. I read that at Office Depot, you can get a will. If the person signs it, and it is notarized, it nullifies all other wills. I was thinking we could put Momma in the car, call Pam, and Janice and all go to see Daddy. We will get him to do a new will. I'm sure he has left everything to some woman who doesn't even matter."

Charlie took a drag from his cigarette, looked over at me, "I don't want anything he has."

I determined that Charlie gets his inheritance, "Charlie, all of us girls are taken care of by our spouses, we are so blessed. You deserve to inherit whatever he has. You're the only son. He never did anything good for any of us, and he needs to make it right. We can at least try." He agreed.

I called Pam and Janice. Leeann was working at her business. I didn't call her; it was hard for her to take time off. Pam drove her Suburban, which accommodated all of us, including Momma's wheelchair. We headed to Birmingham; it was about two hours away.

I called Dad to let him know we were coming., "Is this Charles Perkins?"

"Yes, this is Charlie." He sounded old.

Plastic Tulips in the Winter

"This is Denice, your daughter. Momma, Charlie, Pam, Janice, and I thought we would come to visit you today."

"Well, y'all come on." He gave me directions to his house.

It was a small, red brick house. It had an attached rusty, metal carport and a small front porch that Daddy must have built with some old lumber. Four steps were leading up to the front door, with no stain or paint on the wood. The house was dilapidated.

Sitting in white plastic chairs was two old-looking men. I was not sure which one was Daddy. We pulled up in the dirt driveway, and they both stood up.

Immediately, I knew who Daddy was. The tall man bent over from years of back problems. The wrinkles on his face looked like a road map. His face said it all. He had been run over by life, that's the thing about life, nobody gets a free ride. I could see that he was balding, his hair had turned grey, and his body was thin and frail. His old shiny, worn, dress pants and gathered up, the belt kept them from falling. He had on a white, baggy dress shirt with the sleeves rolled up. It appeared to be a hand-me-down, but I believe he was just so thin, his clothes didn't fit.

A short, chubby, bald man walked down the steps to greet us with a big smile on his face. Charlie got Momma out of the car. Pam, Janice, and I walked over to say hello. I spoke up first. "Hello."

I walked towards him, extending my hand to shake his. "Hey, I'm your Uncle Jeb."

"Uncle Jeb, it's good to see ya."

Momma had always told us about Daddy's brother, Jeb. She said he was a good man. I walked toward the steps and looked at Daddy, he smiled, "Y'all come on in." I noticed he didn't have any teeth.

We quickly got Momma's wheelchair situated in the living room. Daddy walked slowly, bent over as he moved toward his chair, gasping for breath. He sat down in his recliner and put on his oxygen tube that was attached to an oxygen tank placed next to his recliner.

"I had open-heart surgery a few weeks ago." His black dog jumped onto his lap as he continued talking about himself, "I can't breathe. I have to use this oxygen tank."

My eyes began to scan the room. I had a flashback, as a teenager. I had stopped by his house when he was living with his new bride, Marie. Their new furniture was still fresh in my memory. I'm fifty-three, Pam fifty-five, Janice fifty-seven, Charlie forty-six, and Momma, sitting in her wheelchair, was eighty years old. It has been over forty years, and he still had the same furniture.

Daddy's brother was talking about a time when he and his wife were young. "Your Momma took my wife and me to a tent revival, and we accepted Christ as our savior."

I glanced over at Uncle Jeb as he was talking. Momma smiled as she enjoyed the memory. She nodded as he spoke.

I was still scanning the room, amazed to find that things that had seemed so beautiful and expensive were not at all what I had thought. The sofa was cheap, the shiny, two end tables, and matching coffee tables were shiny because they were Formica. They were not real wood. The two matching lamps were cheap metal. The oil painting on the wall was now just a faded print; it was never oil. There stood the same stereo cabinet that played old 45 records, and radio. The brass wall sconces were not brass. They were plastic. They didn't house silk flowers in them. They held plastic. He was sitting in the same green recliner that was not even leather. It was vinyl.

I no longer had the innocent eyes that I once had in my youth; I could now see things as they were. Just like Dad had me as a child, planting plastic tulips in the winter, his house, and life were all plastic. Fake, he always was the great pretender, not the real deal.

My brother Charlie, and Uncle Jeb had pulled chairs up from the kitchen table next to Momma's wheelchair. I grabbed one and pulled it near Daddy. Janice and Pam were sitting on the sofa.

After a few minutes of small talk, I spoke up. "Daddy, since Momma and Charlie were in town visiting, I decided to get all of us together to talk to you about your will. All of us girls are very blessed and taken care of by our husbands."

I looked over at Janice, and pointed toward her, "That is Janice, your oldest child, she is married to a retired Colonel who worked at the Pentagon. Pam is married to a doctor, and I'm married to a minister. Leeann owns her own business, but Charlie has had to stop working to take care of Momma, and we send money every month to help with the expenses. We all agree that it's only right for you to leave everything to Charlie."

He looked at me, "I'm not leaving you, kids, anything. You kids never came to see me. I put all y'all through college, and you never did a thing for me. You kids were never any good. I tried my best with y'all, but you were just no good."

I pulled my chair closer, right up in front of him to get in his face. "Let me tell you, you never paid your child support, and you did not send us to college. You never came around to see us. It was not our responsibility to see you. You were an adult, and we were the children. Only one time I remember you were going to take us for ice cream, and you never showed up, I waited by the window all day. The only time we ever saw you was when you whipped in and out of town with a new woman in the car. You owe Charlie, and you need to make up for your failure as a father."

He responded, "I'm not doing it, you kids were never any good. You're just a bunch of losers. I tried."

Charlie spoke up, "Denice, it doesn't matter," and then Charlie looked at Daddy, "Can I just ask you for something? Can you take your glasses off and let me see the color of your eyes?"

We were all brown-eyed, and Charlie had green eyes. Daddy removed his glasses.

"They're the same as mine, green." He then took Daddy's hands and compared the palms of their hands' side by side as he spoke, "We have the same hands."

I felt a moment of sadness. He was looking for his identity in Daddy. Charlie had never been around Daddy, yet he was built and looked so much like the younger version of Daddy. Charlie had all the charm that Daddy had had at one time, but he was not at all like Daddy. Charlie was an honest, loving, caring man.

I didn't feel Daddy was even worthy of Charlie touching his hand.

I stood and looked directly in his eyes, and with firmness, "Here is the will. Do one thing right in your life for your children. Make everything right at the end of your life."

He responded, "No, I'm not doing anything for you kids." I bent down to make sure we looked eye to eye.

"If you don't do what I'm asking you to do, I will one day look down at you in your coffin, and say, "You never made it right, you never did one good thing toward your children."

Then I stood up to leave, I turned, "and I'm going to leave this will on your table. If you change your mind, our phone numbers are on another paper there."

Plastic Tulips in the Winter

Pam spoke up as she was pulling out of her purse her Polaroid camera, "Daddy, can I get a picture of you?" Pam flashed the image of him in his recliner with his oxygen tube in his nose. Then he stood as we were leaving. She shook his hand with both of her hands, "This is goodbye. I will never see you again."

At that moment, I felt something odd. It was like an electric current went through my body when Pam said that. There was a knowing in me this moment, and her words were final, but then I thought, "How odd, I guess she just needed closure. Her words seemed so final, and matter of fact.

We all walked outside, as Charlie was busy putting Momma, and her wheelchair in the car.

I took Uncle Jeb aside, and told him, "I know you don't know us, and I'm sure we seem like horrible people, but Daddy molested Charlie when he was young, and exposed himself to his daughters. He owes Charlie, and he needs to do this one thing right."

Uncle Jeb looked down at the gravel driveway as he made a groan like he wanted to spit poison out at that news.

"Denice, I know y'all don't know this, but I haven't been around your daddy in years. I don't know him very well. He called me, and said y'all were coming, and bringing your Momma, so I wanted to see her. I do know this one thing; he won't be coming around my children and grandchildren."

"Uncle Jeb, Momma always spoke highly of you."

I wish we had gotten to know him. I could tell he was a wonderful man. He spoke about his children and grandchildren passionately.

We all loaded up in Pam's car to back out of the driveway. She turned the ignition on, looked in her rearview mirror, "Daddy is standing behind the car; I can't back out of the driveway."

Charlie spoke-up, "Jerk, this car in reverse, and run over that, asshole."

We all broke out into laughter. It needed to be said, and Charlie needed to be the one to say it. We are not a family that cusses, but the word did fit. It was as if he had said, "I am above you, and you are beneath me, you're just a dirty spot under my shoe."

Daddy stood broke down from his self-absorbed life, and nothing ever came of that visit.

####

I went back to see him on my own one more time. I didn't care about his will. I needed one last chance to see if there were anything about him that I could find that would change my opinion of him. One last chance on my own, to make sure I had given him every opportunity to show me the decent side of him. I packed my luggage and told Steve I might stay a few days if it went well.

Driving there, I pictured us spending a few days together, laughing, and me telling him about my life, the things I had seen, and done. Maybe he'll look me in the eyes and say something sweet to me, you know, the way I've seen Steve adore our children. I'd tell him about my children and how much I love them. I'd tell him about the foreign countries I've visited, and the wells we put in for villages in Africa that needed water. I could tell him about writing my first novel, and that I've started my second. I thought about what it could be like to have a conversation with my daddy. The kind of things a dad should know about his daughter. I daydreamed all the way to Birmingham of what could be. I arrived at his house, leaving my luggage in the car. I sat with him, and he said the same old things. He told lies about Momma and lies about the women in his life. He talked about how they all used him and left him for other men, how he worked so hard as a provider and tried his best as a dad. He always ended with, "And you know, you kids never were any good. I tried, but you kids were nothing but a disappointment."

While his mouth was moving, I saw a cartoon bubble above his head. It was a skunk telling a bunny rabbit, "You stink." I almost laughed out loud when I saw that. Can you picture that? I told you I'm visual.

I asked him to tell me about his childhood, and that's when he told me about the old-fashioned hoedowns and leaving the country to go into the city. He seemed to enjoy talking about that. I heard he was performing abortions, pretending to be a doctor. How much of that was true, I will never know.

I asked, "How did you become a doctor without getting an education?"

"On the job training." I sat there thinking that if his lips are moving, he's lying.

I asked him if he was ready to meet the Lord. His black dog was in his lap, as he was petting that dog, "Wherever this dog goes, is where I want to be." I looked at that dog, and thought, how strange it was, he loved that dog. Wow.

We went down the road to a country store and got barbecue sandwiches. Dad introduced me to the woman behind the counter, "This is my daughter."

I had never been called that before. It felt strange, a daughter, huh. I dropped him off at his house and then drove a hundred miles home. It was settled, he could never be the daddy I longed for, and it was okay. He did not ever love me, and I was okay with that. I was glad I went to see him. It was to be the last time I saw him alive. And it was okay.

33

Southern Women And Little White Lies

A FEW WEEKS HAD passed. Momma was back in Atlanta with Charlie. Pam, Janice, and I drove to Atlanta to spend the day with her, letting her pick where we were going to eat. Sometimes we stayed overnight at a hotel near Charlie's house.

The three of us enjoyed the drive to Atlanta, and one of us would always start a story which we called, Southern Women, and Little White Lies. We made up stories about a small little Southern town. It had an ice-cream parlor, beauty parlor, post office, and the corner drug store. There was the First Methodist Church that most people attended in the town, where they showed up in their Sunday best.

We spoke Southern, with a deep Southern lazy drawl, as we told our made-up stories. There were the two old-maid sisters, retired schoolteachers. They served Papa's recipe in their china teacups and talked about the Civil War, and how they had hidden their silver trays, and candlesticks under the front porch.

We had many Southern women in this made-up town and told the latest scandal going on in their lives. We laughed so hard we cried as we interrupted each other to add our part of the gossip. I always brought the town slut into the story. Being a pastor's wife, I just wasn't given to gossip and calling people sluts, and whores. However, I had a lot of fun talking about her with my sisters.

I told them, "The men at the barbershop named her the town bicycle because everyone gets a ride." Pam and Janice screamed out in laughter when I talked about her entering the corner drug store or a beauty parlor. She made sure she always showed up.

I understand that a preacher's wife should not speak like this, but it was just between us sisters. It was fun and a wonderful memory of our times together.

It was one of these trips when Pam told us something that happened to her the week before. "I received a phone call from one of my friends. Her husband is the owner, and CEO of a huge corporation," She continued, "You know how Southern she is, very slow, and soft-spoken." Well, she told me, "Pam, I did something, and I am so ashamed, but Pam, I had to call you and tell you what I did."

Pam asked, "Savannah Gail, what did you do?"

"You know it's Christmas, and again it is time for our annual Christmas party for the company. My husband informed me I was not welcome this year, but that I had to prepare my special Christmas punch recipe. You know my punch is always the hit of the party."

She went on to say, "Pam, I knew why I wasn't invited this year. My husband had an affair with that slut of a secretary in his office. He informed me he would take the Christmas punch to the party.

Pam, I pulled out my fine crystal punch bowl that my grandmother left me. I began to mix my special recipe. I thought about not being included, and that slut of a whore would be standing around my crystal punch bowl, drinking my punch.

Well, I just felt faint at the thought of it. I walked over to my cupboard and pulled out a teacup. You know my fine china, the one my grandmother left me in her will. Well, Pam, I hate to tell you, but Pam, I declare, I peed in that teacup and added it to the punch."

Pam gasped, "Savannah Gail, you didn't?"

"Oh, yes, I did, and he left with the punch bowl and my special recipe. I went into my master bathroom, put on my beautiful long sexy nightgown, the black lace one he gave me for our anniversary. I fixed my hair and make-up and put on my favorite perfume. I turned on romantic music, lit a fire in the fireplace, and poured me a glass of the finest red wine. I relaxed in front of that fire, picturing that party around my punch bowl with that slut drinking my Christmas punch. Pam, I could hardly contain myself with laughter. It was the most marvelous evening around the fire.

"Well, my husband walked in after the party, carrying the empty punch bowl." "Savannah Gail, as usual, your punch was the hit of the Christmas Party." "He was grinning from ear to ear. You know that smirky gorilla grin he has."

I smiled, "I'm so glad they enjoyed it, and did you have some yourself?"

"Of course, I did. I love your punch recipe."

As I sipped on my wine, "Well, that's just marvelous. I'm so happy you had some yourself."

He went to go shower while I poured another glass of wine. I was very relaxed. I guess a little tipsy. I kid you not. I felt powerful. It was a most definitely triumphant feeling."

Plastic Tulips in the Winter

"Do you think I'm a bad person, Pam? Do you think I'm bad to the bone?"

Janice and I were screaming with laughter while Pam was telling us about this real incident.

Southern women have a way about them. An air about them that they are made of fine china. Though the surface may look like fine china, underneath there is a she-devil is waiting to be released. When push comes to shove, a Southern woman will leave you scratched and bleeding every time.

We continued to make memories with Momma. Pam, Janice, Leeann, and I took her to see New York. We all met at the airport in Montgomery. I got out of the car with a jam box playing a CD real loud, so Momma could hear it. It was Frank Sinatra singing, "New York, New York." We rented a limo in New York and had the limo driver play it for Momma. She wiggled in her seat, moving to the music.

During that time, my Misty went through a divorce. We stood beside our daughter to hold her up in her pain. I still find it peculiar how people are so quick to judge and whisper instead of praying. I learned that until you've walked in someone else's shoes, keep silent and pray. There were people, Steve and I stood with over the years during their time of trouble, yet they whispered about my daughter. I just can't relate to that kind of friend, but I forgave them in my heart. Life is good. We choose to look forward to the future and not back to the past that we cannot change.

"As a man thinketh in his heart, so is he". Proverbs 23:7

I HAVE LEARNED:

With the paintbrush my thoughts, and the canvas of my mind, I paint a beautiful picture of my future.

Life is Beautiful that way.

#PlasticTulips

34

It's Your Hormones

ONE EVENING, as I was in the kitchen making a big pot of homemade chili for supper, I noticed Pam pull up to my house. It wasn't unusual for her to drop by, but the look on her face as she opened the door told me something was wrong. I turned the burner down low so that we could talk. "What's up?"

I placed two glasses of sweet tea down on the table for us to drink. Pam sat down and took a sip. Her bottom lip quivered as she struggled to hold back her tears. I asked again, "Pam, what's wrong?"

She paused, looked down at her glass of tea, giving much thought to her next words, "Denice, I think I'm going to die."

"Pam, why do you feel this?" I asked with concern.

"I don't know, Denice. I just do." She began to cry.

I reached over to comfort her and told her she might be having a hormone imbalance or depression. Maybe it was as simple as getting on hormone pills or an antidepressant.

"It's just a feeling, a sense inside of me that I'm going to die."

I began to rebuke her. I reminded her of what the Bible says about the power of the tongue. "Pam, you know the Bible says, I set before you, Life, and Death. Choose you which way you will go." She looked at me with trust as she said, "I know you're right."

Pam was a real intercessor, and she could hear from God. It bothered me. Pam did not live in fear, not at all. She was delivered years ago, and she trusted God.

I told her, "Now, you go tomorrow, and see your doctor. Get him to check your hormones and talk to him about putting you on an antidepressant. Do you hear me, Pam?" We prayed together, and that was that. She wiped away her tears with her Kleenex and nodded her head in agreement.

"Maybe you're right; it's my hormones."

"You're going to be all right, Pam," I assured her.

Plastic Tulips in the Winter

####

A few months later, Pam told me, "Denice, I have trouble driving, staying in the lane."

She said her husband didn't want her to drive anymore until she found out what her problem was. I told her, "Pam, that sounds like you may be having inner ear problems, like vertigo. You need to go to an ENT doctor."

I was off my feet for five weeks, because I had just had foot surgery. Rheumatoid arthritis had curled my toes and I had them straightened with pins that were sticking out of each toe. I had to keep my feet propped up as I watched TV all day.

Pam could get right in to see an ENT. Pam and Janice stopped by to see me after the appointment, informing me that he wanted Pam to have a brain scan.

My response was, "That makes sense." No big deal to me, just good sense.

Later that evening, I had just finished my bath when the phone rang. It was Janice, "Denice, Pam has something seriously wrong."

I responded, "Why are you thinking that? It's going to be vertigo." Janice was always a drama queen, so I was not going to let her go there.

I was still on week four of staying off my foot, so Janice took Pam for the brain scan. They came to my house after they had gone to lunch, and Pam still had no answers. That afternoon Pam's husband received a call from the doctor.

"I need you, and Pam at my office tomorrow morning."

The next day after they met with the doctor, Pam called me and told me there was a tumor on her brain, and that the doctor wants her to get a full-body PET scan. I immediately called Janice.

"Denice, I told you," she responded.

I then said back to her, "Everything is going to be all right, Janice." My insides shook to the core as I realized Pam was in trouble. This can't be happening. Janice took Pam for her PET scan.

The doctor called again, requesting Pam and her husband to come to his office. That afternoon after the appointment, they came straight to my house. They both sat down as Pam pulled a Kleenex out of her purse. She began to fold it into that perfect square she always made, and then a triangle to catch her tears. Her husband began to tell me that cancer had started in her pancreas and had spread to her brain. She had pancreatic cancer and a brain tumor.

Plastic Tulips in the Winter

As those words came out of his mouth. Pam was catching her tears from the corners of her eyes with her handkerchief. She looked helpless at that moment. Her husband was still talking while my mind was trying to take it all in. Pancreatic cancer and brain tumor were overwhelming words. I thought to myself, I'm not hearing this. This is not real, I screamed in silence, MY GOD!

He continued, "The doctor says the brain tumor will take her before cancer in the pancreas. She has eight to twelve weeks to live if left untreated. If treated, they might be able to give her a year to a year and a half."

I was taken back, no, no, no. Pam wiped her eyes as her bottom lip quivered. She cried quietly, and then she spoke in a weak, trembling voice, "If they can only give me a year, I'm not going to have treatment."

Fight rose within me. I looked at Pam, "We know how to fight this battle. Pam, we have been here before with Momma. God will do it again for us. We are not quitters. We know who our God is." She wept; she nodded her head, agreeing, with me, wiping away her tears.

I looked at her, "Pam, you will get treatment, and you will live and not die. God will make a way of escape for you. We will beat this; you will fight, and there will be no giving up. We will look the world over for a cure. We will beat this." I declared.

They both agreed. Pam and her husband went home. Steve was out of town, and I was in shock. I had a gut feeling; it was a knowing in my soul. She was not going to beat this; this was a battle; we were not going to win.

When Momma was told she was dying of cancer, there was a gift of faith present, but this one was different. There was a knowing that the supernatural faith was not there. It's hard to explain until you have walked in it. It's not a button you can push. It is there for the battle or it is not.

I picked up the phone and called the church. All our adult children worked in the ministry with us. I called Brian, my son-in-law. "Brian, come home." I screamed and hung up the phone. That's all I could say. Within minutes they were all pulling up into the driveway. My daughters Stacy, Misty, and Denice, with their spouses, along with Stephen, and his wife Hillary.

Stacy ran in, "Momma, what's wrong?"

I could see the look of fear on her face as she asked. They all thought that I was going to tell them their daddy was dead. Steve was flying his plane, and their first thought was that I was going to say there had been a plane crash. My children had never seen me like this. I was doubled over in my chair, screaming a blood-curdling scream until I thought my head was going to burst as I talked through the horror of the moment.

"Pam, Pam is dying."

An overwhelming feeling of hopelessness came over me, as I spoke the word "dying." I screamed, I cried. I covered my face with my hands, trying to muffle the screams. I had a flashback of her shaking Daddy's hand. "This is goodbye. I will never see you again." I remember when she came walking into my kitchen, crying, "Denice, I think I'm going to die."

My kids were crying for Pam. They were crying because the mother, who had always been so strong, was folded over in despair. I cried from my gut. My children left. I called Janice, "Janice, Pam is dying." I was still crying.

"Denice, I told you it was bad."

"My God, Janice, this can't be happening."

Janice said she would go by Leeann's store to tell her, and I called Charlie. He began to sob over the phone.

"Charlie, I'm coming to Atlanta in the morning to see my foot doctor and get these pins taken out, so I can walk. Please don't tell Momma until I get there. I couldn't bear the thought of her told her daughter was going to die before her.

I called Daddy to tell him the bad news.

"Daddy, I called because I felt you should know that one of your children has cancer and is going to die."

"Which one?" he asked.

"It's Pam, Daddy,"

His response was, "Well, I haven't been feeling very well lately, myself."

"Do you understand what I just told you? One of your children is going to die."

He answered, "Ever since I had my heart bypass surgery, I just haven't felt good either."

"Dad, when I was a little girl, I remember thinking you were a fool, and now I'm in my fifties, and I realize you are still a fool, just an old fool. I will never call you again." I hung up.

I don't know why, but I still wanted to think he would care. It just wasn't in him to care. My mind could not comprehend a parent, not feeling pain with the news that their child is dying.

I HAVE LEARNED:

LIFE will deal you cards that you do not think you can handle.

You may feel all alone.

BUT

God is still there, walking beside you!

#PlasticTulips

PAM

One-year before she passed away.

PAM AND MOM

35

Remember This Moment

THE NEXT MORNING, I explained to my foot doctor why he had to take the pins out early. I wore a special boot for a few more weeks. I went straight to Charlie's house. Momma was sitting in the living room; I wasn't sure if Charlie had already told her.

Pulling a footstool up close to her, "Momma, Pam has some bad news." She looked at me.

"Mom, the doctors found a brain tumor. It's cancer in Pam's brain and pancreas. They have given her eight to twelve weeks left to live."

Momma lifted her hand in the air with her face tilted upward as she declared, "God, my baby, my baby! God, my baby," she moaned a moan deep and unbearable; it pierced my soul.

Then she made her declaration, "God, I trust you, I trust you, God." She made her hand into a fist toward heaven, saying again, "I trust you, God."

I knew Pam was not going to make it. "Momma, if Pam goes before you, Pam will be there waiting for you, to show you heaven."

She nodded, "Yes." Trembling in her wheelchair like the wind has been knocked out of her. We held hands as we prayed together, and then I grabbed her face between my hands, kissing it all over. "I love you, Momma."

"Janice, Pam, and I will not be coming to Atlanta. We'll be busy taking Pam to her treatments."

Mom spoke up, "I will come to see y'all."

On my drive back to Montgomery, I called Janice on my cell phone. We agreed that together, we would take Pam for her chemo and brain radiation treatments. We agreed she would not be allowed to be alone for one moment. I couldn't stand the idea of her being awake, alone in the house with her thoughts. Janice and I agreed that together, we would walk this journey with Pam.

Plastic Tulips in the Winter

During this time, Steve and I were having our house remodeled, and we needed to move out. Therefore, we rented a house at Lake Martin. We knew it would be peaceful on the lake. Every morning, Steve and I would drive to Montgomery, and I would meet up with Janice at Pam's house.

When I arrived at Pam's, her housekeeper was working in the kitchen, and Pam was either soaking in her garden tub or putting on make-up, getting herself ready to go out for the day.

Her doctor had said the brain tumor would take Pam before cancer in the pancreas. Pancreatic cancer is the most painful death, and the tumor in the brain could be a blessing.

Pam decided to fight. She began treatment, attempting to shrink the tumor on the brain with radiation therapy followed by intravenous (IV) Chemotherapy to attack cancer in the rest of her body.

We understood these treatments would only give her months to a year to live. It was not going to be a cure. I spent most of my nights awake, praying for God to provide us with a miracle, trying to connect with faith. Faith that had a knowing, God, was going to pull this off, a miracle. I just couldn't get it. I would fall asleep at night, and after only a few hours of sleep, I woke up with the horrible thought, "Pam's dying, oh, God, no."

It was a hopeless feeling. I searched the Internet looking for a cure. I knew she was dying, but she was not dead yet.

Everyday Janice, Pam, and I drove to the cancer treatment center for Pam's treatment or to see her doctor. There were times she was so weak she had to walk arm in arm between us, prompting the memory of us, as we slept like children. Pam wrapped her arms and legs over and around us so she could sleep without fear. Here we were again. This time the boogeyman was going to get her, and we knew it. My God help us; we are so fragile. I felt her slipping out of our hands. I was smothering, but I couldn't show it. She was my sister. I didn't want to be strong. I felt my world was caving in as the ground gave way under my feet. God help me take my next breath.

One morning, as I was sitting on the side of the garden tub talking to Pam while she shampooed her hair, she began to pour the freshwater over her head with a plastic container. Loose hair fell into the tub. Pam touched her head, and a hand full of hair came out into her hand. She started crying, holding her hair in her hand.

Plastic Tulips in the Winter

"Pam, you're so beautiful, just put on some big earrings, and strut your stuff."

She said, "I guess I should go to my hairdresser and get her to shave it off."

"I'll get her to shave me, too."

"Oh no, you won't," she responded firmly. "If you shave your head, you will be the only bald one. I'm going to get me a wig."

I laughed, "Let's do it today.

We found a wig that looked just like her real hair, and a second wig that was far from who she was. A long blonde straight wig fell to the middle of her back. It was very sexy, not at all Pam's usual classy style. She was fifty-five years old, but she wore it out in public anyway. She got a kick out of it. It was as if to say, "What does it matter? I'll just have fun with it. Who cares what people think?" I knew people in the city would find Pam's choice in wigs a little daring, but Janice, and I enjoyed every moment of her wearing it.

Every day, the same conversation came up between Janice and Pam.

Janice would say, "Now, Pam, if you don't get your miracle and you take your last breath. When you start going toward the light, I want you to choose to come back. We will be standing over you, asking God to give you back, to put you back into your body."

Pam agreed not to go toward the light. She always said, "I'm not going to have to do that because I'm not going to die, Janice."

Janice brought that up, and sometimes Pam would stop her in the middle of the conversation and say, "I know, I know. Don't run toward the light."

We all laughed because this was a conversation in the middle of lunch or while at the mall as we looked through racks of clothes, pointing out cute tops to each other. We did not care if people overheard our conversation, what they may think. This was our time together; sisters. We were living this moment the way we chose. Life can be beautiful that way when you are truly free of the fear of people.

Again, Janice would ask her, "Now, what do you do as you feel yourself going toward the light?" Pam would respond, "I don't go to the light." It was like they were studying for a test.

We spent days getting her treatment and then shopping until we dropped. We returned to Pam's house in time to watch TV until her husband came home from his office.

Plastic Tulips in the Winter

Sometimes Pam would feel weak, and she would go to bed. She always wanted Janice to tuck her in. Pam in her pretty pajamas, and a pair of white socks to keep her feet warm. She would go over to the bed, and carefully, in an elegant way, perform the same routine. Pull the corner of her bedspread back, and then take the edge of her sheet, pulling it again even with the spread, and then smoothing the sheet with her hand. You know, the way hotels do when they fix your bed for you in the evenings.

This day, as Pam lay down on the bed, she waited for Janice to pull the cover over her. I think Pam didn't want to do it because she might get her pajamas wrinkled, and Pam liked Janice babying her anyway. Janice pulled the sheet up under Pam's chin, and then the bedspread just like Pam wanted it.

This time Janice grabbed a pillow and started going with it toward her face saying, "Now, I'm going to send you to Jesus, close your eyes," she said, laughing.

Pam pushed it away from her face laughing, "Quit it, Janice." The three of us laughed. Janice was always joking with Pam.

Pam thought Janice was one of the funniest people. Janice always made us laugh. We would be sitting in a restaurant, and a beautiful young girl with an excellent figure walk by, Janice would look her up, and down, and say, "She makes me sick." We cracked up laughing.

Anyway, while Janice tucked Pam in, I noticed Pam had an eight by ten photo frame of Momma on her nightstand and sitting on top of it in the left-hand corner of the frame was the four by six black white Polaroid photo she took of Daddy the last time she saw him.

I asked her, "Why do you have his picture by your bed?"

She looked at it, "So I will remember to pray for him. I wonder if he knows I'm sick."

I looked at her and was honest with her. "I called, and told Dad, Pam."

"What did he say?" She looked at me with a look of hope that he cared, like a little girl.

"He said he hadn't been feeling well himself. It was all about him. He will never change, Pam."

The corners of her mouth turned down as she rolled her eyes, "It doesn't matter."

"Nope, he doesn't matter. He doesn't care about us, and we sure don't need him."

####

That night while I was up late searching the Internet for a cure for Pam, God spoke to me to tell Pam something. So, I did the next morning. "Pam, the Lord told me to tell you, do not go into dark places in your mind." She began to cry as she sat in the tub.

"That helps me so much, from this day forward, I will not think of dying. I trust God. If he chooses to take me, I am at peace. I'm ready to meet Him face to face, but I do not believe I'm going to die. I'm not afraid to die. I know I will be with God. I will not go into dark places in my mind." Her lips quivered.

PAM'S FINAL CHAPTER

Pam walked this final chapter in her life as brave as anyone could have. There was no fear. She was at total peace with God. As a child, she had feared the grave, but now she walked this last walk with no fear, in complete peace, resting in the arms of God.

Steve came by many times to take communion and pray with her. He gave her a CD by Sarah McLachlan, "In the Arms of the Angel." She would stand as he gave her communion as she silently cried.

Pam's five children were all grown. Four were married with children of their own, and her youngest was at college in Savannah, Georgia. Pam didn't want her to quit school, but it was hard on her daughter. She called her mother, three, and four times a day. All Pam's kids would check on her during the day, and her oldest son, while on his lunch break, would find us wherever we were.

We called Leeann to meet us for lunch at least every other day. She always came even though she was busy with her business.

The holidays were here, Janice had a large home on six acres of land with an indoor pool, circle shape game room, with four jukeboxes she called her 50s room. It had a pool table, and a couple of arcade machines, a bar, and an antique booth.

Her open family room and the kitchen had a stone fireplace. She and Tom set up tables to hold all of us. The number varied between forty-five and fifty-five, which included Momma's grandchildren and great-grandchildren. Babies were crying, toddlers were running around, and the teens were enjoying the 50s room.

The men enjoyed Tom's gun collection. They got out on their land to shoot, while the women were all getting the food ready. There was always plenty of food, and desserts. Usually, one of the teens had invited a boyfriend or girlfriend to join us.

This Thanksgiving was different. There was the unspoken reality that Pam may not be at the table with us next year. She chose not to wear her wig that day because it would feel hot and tight on her head. She had a beautiful silk scarf wrapped around her head tied in the back. Her make-up was perfect. She wore her two diamond rings, and diamond stud earrings.

After we finished our meal, we sat with our coffee and dessert, talking for hours. Pam did the unveiling of her scarf to show anyone who had not seen her baldhead. We laughed, not at her, but with her. We looked at her beautiful face as she laughed with us.

I had the thought, "Maybe I should have let her polish me up," but I don't know, I liked just being me. I felt sorrow and a sense of deep sadness as I looked at her. As she looked over at me, I tried to cover my thoughts with a smile. It was painful. I heard my soul say, "Remember this moment, she won't be with you next Thanksgiving." I knew we all were thinking the same thing, and we knew Pam was having the same thoughts. Oh! I am going to miss her.

I HAVE LEARNED:

Family, what a powerful army it can be. United in our love for each other.

#PlasticTulips

36

Sista Hat

NEW YEAR'S WAS around the corner, and the church always put on a big celebration with skits, balloons, and noisemakers. Our church congregation was large, and it had a substantial African American population. I always joked with them to wear their favorite hat, what I called their "Sista-Hats."

I had a jacket made of ribbons. It was every bright color you can imagine. I always got compliments on it. It was wired with tiny Christmas lights powered by batteries. You couldn't see the wires or the lights. I just pushed the button, and I lit up. I added battery-operated lights to my "Sista-Hat." It always made the congregation laugh when I walked up on the platform.

We went shopping for hats, and we took Momma with us to the Burlington Coat Factory. Walking in, pushing Mom in her wheelchair, "Let's go to the hats.

I've got to get a new "Sista-Hat" for the New Year's Eve Celebration."

The department store music was playing Justin Timberlake, Sexy Back. I grabbed a candy apple red hat. It looked like a roller coaster on top of it with a red satin bow on the side. I placed it on Mom's head as Janice wrapped a cobalt blue long string of feathers around Momma's neck. Pam grabbed elbow-length black gloves to put on her. As Justin was singing about bringing sexy back, I began to spin her wheelchair around, moving to the beat of the music as she laughed, she gave her queens wave in the air.

People were walking by, stopping to watch the beautiful lady in a wheelchair as we danced around her, laughing. She loved all the attention we gave her. We had fun that day it made a great memory

####

The holidays came and went. It was now March. Every summer, Pam and her husband took all their married children and grandchildren to their beach house in Destin, Florida, where Janice and Leeann also owned beach homes. It was a family time every summer in June, just for them.

We had just taken Pam for her treatment and had grabbed a bite to eat at one of Pam's favorite restaurants next door to the Burlington Coat Factory. Pam had mentioned she needed to go there to find some new summer sandals for their vacation in June. Janice and I knew Pam wouldn't be going on that family vacation. Pam loved shoes—high heels, flats, and sandals. She had tiny feet and always kept them manicured.

She had times when she became confused, and this was one of those days. She got excited and went up and down the aisles trying on shoes and then placing them in her buggy. Janice and I pulled them out and put them back on the shelves. We expressed excitement over each pair she tried on. Janice and I laughed as we pulled them out of the buggy.

Pam kept asking, "What are y'all laughing about?"

"Oh, nothing, Denice is acting crazy. I'm just laughing at her."

I said, "Let's go to another department. You already have plenty of shoes." She found two bathing suits and a pair of shorts.

"Pam, it's getting late. Let's go pay for this and get back to your house so you can rest." Unloading her buggy at the register, she found only two pairs of sandals.

"Hmm, that's strange. I could have sworn I found more than two pairs."

I said, "No. Remember, you put them back."

She nodded, "That's right."

We took Pam home. Her housekeeper informed her that Walt would come by to see her later, Pam smiled. She loved seeing her sons. Her younger son, Cameron, would come by in the mornings, and make her some hot tea. They loved their Momma.

Pam headed toward her bedroom, "Janice, come tuck me in bed."

"Ok, come on, let me tuck my baby in bed."

Janice loved every minute of it. She took Pam through her routine, and then she walked back into the living room where I was having a glass of sweet tea.

Janice sat down on the sofa, looked over at me, "I'm studying every little thing about her. I observe her every minute of the day. When we sit across from each other, I study her face, her expressions, and the way Pam holds her teacup as she sips her hot tea, the way she takes little bites and chews forever before she swallows. Every move is so dainty, feminine, and full of grace. I will remember everything about her. I'm taking in every moment."

Plastic Tulips in the Winter

I listened to Janice and responded, "I know." That's all I could reply. What I did not say to Janice was that I wanted to fall on the floor, curl up like a baby, and scream out, "No, no, no." I wanted to yell at the heavens and make the earth shake with my cry to God. I couldn't believe life was dealing us these cards. I cannot save her. Life isn't fair.

####

Janice caught a bad cold and was going to stay home a few days. We knew she didn't need to be around Pam.

I decided to talk to Pam about things she should take care of.

"Pam, I was thinking about myself, and how important it is to update wills, and what things I would leave to each of my children. This is not to say you are going to die, but don't you think this is something you should do?"

She responded, "I don't want to think about that."

I accepted that as her answer and was going to leave it alone.

The next afternoon her oldest daughter Melissa came by. Pam had just taken a bath and was putting her pajamas on. Melissa and I were sitting on the bed, talking as Pam took off her wig, and tied her silk scarf around her head.

"Melissa," Pam said, "I want to show you these diamond earrings I am going to leave you one day."

Pam went over to her jewelry box, pulled out a tiny white box, and reached in to pull out her long string of diamond earrings she had worn to a southern ball. After Pam showed them to her, she went back into her bathroom to put face cream on.

I whispered to her, "Go find a pen and some paper." Pam walked back into the bedroom.

I asked, "What about all of your diamond rings, and your minks? Which daughter gets which mink?" She went over to her closet and pulled her mink coats out, "Melissa, you can have this full-length black sable, and then she pulled out two more minks for the other two daughters."

"Pam, Melissa is going to write all this down."

Pam knew what I was up to. She calmly began to pull out all her expensive jewelry, showing Melissa, and telling her which child, it was to be left to. She wanted her two son's spouses to receive a piece of jewelry, too. Melissa wrote it all down. Pam told

Melissa of a savings account she wanted all five children to split.

I was so proud of Melissa; she wasn't crying as Pam pulled the items out. She took notes as if she were a secretary. Pam told Melissa that if she went on to be with the Lord, she wanted Melissa to see to it that when her little sister falls in love and marries that she takes Pam's place to help her plan the wedding of her dreams. Pam's other two daughters had beautiful Southern weddings. I could tell Pam was glad she and Melissa took care of that.

I HAVE LEARNED:

TEARS are for the Moment,
BUT
MEMORIES are for a Lifetime.

#PlasticTulips

I HAVE LEARNED:

Memories must be made.
They take only a few
seconds of your day but
last a lifetime.

#PlasticTulips

37

God, Help Us

THE NEXT MORNING, I was driving Pam to the Cancer Center for her IV treatment. She was weak and thin. She didn't bother to put on any make-up with a silk scarf tied on her head. As we walked to the car, she walked slumped over, and slow. As I put the car in drive, pulling away from her house, "Denice, tell me about God."

I began to remind her of what a big God we serve. As I was, listening to myself talk to her, I was thinking how tired and emotionally drained I felt. I hear myself talking about our big, God, and I am thinking, "Oh, God, hear my words, touch my starving soul, feed my spirit God. I need a recharge from you that only you can give."

However, I kept telling her about God. "Remember, years ago, we went to hear Betty Baxter share the miracle she received in her body?"

She answered in a weak voice, "Tell me again about her miracle."

I began to tell Pam the story. "Betty was born with a disease that had made her an invalid, and her body was all twisted. God told her and her mother that He was going to come and perform a miracle on a particular day at three o'clock in the afternoon. They knew the date and time that He was going to do this. The day came, and her mother propped Betty on pillows by the window in a big chair. Betty had on a new pair of shoes her daddy had bought for her. She'd never worn shoes before. A few family friends from church and her pastor were there along with her Momma, daddy, and baby brother. They waited for God to come at three o'clock."

Pam opened her purse, and pulled out a Kleenex, laying it flat on one of her legs, she began to fold it into a perfect square, and then a triangle. I had seen her do that so many times in an organized manner. She took one corner of the triangle to wipe away the tears as they ran down her cheek.

She silently cried as I continued talking.

I continued, "The curtains began to blow through the open window. Betty said to her Momma, 'He's here!'

Plastic Tulips in the Winter

Suddenly, every bone in her body began to snap into place." I looked at Pam, "Pam, God can heal you!"

She nodded, "Tell me more about God, Denice."

As I drove, I continued telling her about the love of God, and how He cares for her. How powerful our God is. "Pam, God loves you." She shook her head in agreement.

But every emotion inside of me was stirring in agony. I wanted to yell to the heavens that this isn't fair, my sister is dying, but I remained calm. I continued telling her about the love of God.

We finished at the treatment center, and as usual, we went to eat. Pam was quiet, so I carried the conversation at the table. I told her that she seemed tired today, and we shouldn't go shopping. "No," she said. "I want to go to Dillard's Department store." She said there was something she needed to get. Pam usually wanted make-up or perfume.

We got out of the car, but she was so weak. I put my arm through hers to help her walk. We stood in the cosmetic department, and I asked her whether it was lipstick, blush, or eyeliner.

"I think it is upstairs." We took the escalator up.

"Let's go over to the linen department."

We stood in the department, but she couldn't get her thoughts together. The saleswoman walked up, "May I help you?"

"Yes, my sister wants to buy something,"

The saleswoman asks, "Ma'am, is it bed sheets you want?"

I looked at the woman and could see she was quickly assessing Pam. So, to protect my sister, "Pam, the chemo has made you tired."

Then I saw a look of understanding on the woman's face.

Pam said she would not leave until she found what she had come for. The woman began to show her towels and bath rugs. "It is made of marble."

The saleswoman responded, "I know what it is." I immediately knew myself. Over the ten months of our shopping, Pam had seen me look at the toothbrush holder, cup holder, hand pump, and soap dish, all in red onyx marble that matched the red onyx marble I was having installed on my new master bathroom countertops. The marble trashcan alone cost ninety dollars, one toothbrush holder was around thirty dollars, and I needed two for two sinks. The salesperson showed it to her. "That's it."

Plastic Tulips in the Winter

"I'm not going to let you buy that."

"I want the whole set, with two toothbrush holders. This is for you, Denice." I decided just to let her buy me the trashcan for my memory with her. I took her home and put her to bed.

THE BEGINNING OF THE END

The next morning when I arrived, Pam was still in bed asleep. We couldn't wake her. We spent all day going into her room, checking on her. We called her name, but nothing woke her. So, we just let her sleep.

The following day I was able to wake her. I took her to her doctor's appointment without Janice. I dressed her in her beige linen pants and a short sleeve, mint green blouse. She didn't bother to put her blonde wig on. She tied her silk scarf on her head, no make-up, and no jewelry.

It began to rain as we walked towards the car. I noticed she was thinner, and the color of her skin was turning yellower. The whites of her eyes were no longer white; they were yellow. I knew that was a sign of her liver shutting down. She walked slumped forward instead of walking with the perfect posture I was used to seeing. To my horror, I noticed her pants were wet. I wanted to cry. "Pam, your slacks are wet, let's go back inside, and change clothes."

She mumbled, "No, let's just go. It doesn't matter."

It hurt to see her perfectly pressed slacks with a big wet spot on the seat. At any other time in her life, she would not have let anyone see her like this. She would have gone back into the house to change. However, I couldn't convince her to go back inside.

The nurse saw Pam as we walked in and took us straight to a room. Pam sat slumped on the patient table and didn't say a word. I told the doctor about the changes I was observing in Pam. Pam didn't speak. She just seemed very cloudy in her ability to focus her eyes and think.

"Doctor, she didn't wake up yesterday. We tried to wake her, but there was no response. Her bowels have not moved in days, and she doesn't want to drink anything because she chokes. I tried to make her drink some water, but she couldn't swallow, so she spits it out in a bowl."

He looked at Pam, put out his hand to take her hand in his. "I'm so sorry, Mrs. Williams, this is the beginning of the end." He tenderly let go of her hand and walked out of the room.

I was stunned, I wanted more from the doctor, but I realized he dealt with cancer patients every day, and this was his way of dealing with it.

Plastic Tulips in the Winter

I lifted Pam off the table and grabbed her purse. I wrapped my arm through her arm to support her. "Pam, come on." We walked to the car, arm in arm.

As I drove away, she turned to me and asked in a weak voice, "What did he mean by that?" I just couldn't say it. I couldn't tell her what he meant.

I responded, "I don't know, that was strange, wasn't it?" I took her home and put her to bed.

That evening Steve could tell I was down. I was quiet. He suggested we get in the boat and go for a ride on the lake. As he drove, I went to the back of the boat. I began to cry, I screamed, it echoed across the lake. My heart was being ripped out of me.

Steve asked, "Are you okay?" He drove fast across the lake so that I could cry and scream, where no one could hear me. He knew I needed a release. I grabbed a green towel to muffle the sound of my screams. I wept and screamed until I could cry no more. Steve took me back to the cabin and put me to bed.

The next morning, driving back into town, I began to cry again. Doubled over in my seat, I wailed in agony. Through my tears, "Take me to the emergency room, Steve, I think I'm having a nervous breakdown; I can't stop crying."

He drove as fast as he could; and just kept looking over at me, as I cried out loud, he was praying out loud. It was a forty-five-minute drive from the lake to Montgomery. By the time we got into town, I had taken control of myself and had him drop me off at Pam's. She was still asleep.

Janice was over the flu, and already there. I went in, sat in Pam's den, and watched television. Pam's housekeeper was in the kitchen cleaning.

Janice came into the den. "Denice, Pam wants to talk to you."

I sat on the side of the bed next to her. "Pam, what is it?" Her voice was thick because she could no longer swallow fluids.

"I need to tell you something."

I leaned in closer with the fear she would not be able to finish, and I would never know what she wanted to tell me. I asked, "Pam, what is it?"

"I need to tell you something. I need to tell you something," Pam kept saying it over and over.

"Pam, try to tell me." Slowly, she pushed the air out with her words, "I don't want to leave my body."

"Do you want me to pray, Pam?"

Struggling to push out her words, "Yes."

Plastic Tulips in the Winter

Kneeling next to her bed, I laid my hands on her chest and began to pray out loud. "God, please God, please, God, please," I begged.

I prayed. "God, let Pam stay. You are a mighty and powerful God. You, God, changed all our lives. We know you, and we know your power. You are our healer, our savior. I'm asking you to leave Pam with us. Change your mind about this God. You're our only hope. You're our only answer. You are a mighty God, and you are a powerful God; I look to only you. We need your help. You are God of all our lives. All powerful and mighty God, hear me now as I cry out to you."

I leaned close to Pam, and asked, "Pam, can you hear me? Did you hear mc praying?"

She whispered, "Yes, pray louder." I prayed again, pleading my case with God.

She drifted off into a deep sleep again. I went back into the living room to let her sleep. For two more days, she was in and out of sleep.

At one point, Janice and I walked in and sat on the bed looking at her.

She opened her eyes, looked at Janice, and me. She smiled, "If you could see what I'm seeing, you would be jealous."

I asked, "Are you seeing angels?"

She whispered, "Yes."

Janice looked at her, "I am jealous; you always did have to be first." I just looked at Janice, shook my head, and smiled at her.

CALL HOSPICE

We called Hospice; they came. Janice and I explained to the two nurses that Pam had been active until a few days ago. "This is the process of her shutting down," they explained."

While we were talking, to my surprise, Pam walked into the room with her eyes wide open and alert. She sat down on the sofa next to me. My mouth fell open with shock for a moment to see that kind of strength after Pam had been weak and asleep for days.

We explained to Pam, who the nurses were. "Pam, they are from Hospice."

In a matter of fact way, "I know."

She sat proper, as she always did as they began to ask her questions. Answering them as calmly and lady-like as if she were at a job interview. "Mrs. Pam, are you fine with us checking in on you every day?"

Pam answered, "Yes."

Then I showed them out and walked over to Pam. I sat down on the edge of the coffee table in front of her. Taking her by the hands, I begin to cry, "I don't want you to go, I don't want you to die," I fell to my knees, burying my head in her lap sobbing.

Slow, and distinct, "Denice, I'm not going to die."

I looked up at her, "Pam, you are, and if we don't get a miracle, you're going to die soon. You're going to be with the Lord, Pam." I cried from my soul. I didn't want her to leave without us saying goodbye.

Slowly in a whisper, "Denice, I am not going to die." I knew she knew she was dying, but she saw it as stepping over to a life in heaven. Pam had peace. I sobbed with my head in her lap. She caressed the back of my head to comfort me, rubbing my hair. I then put her to bed.

MY BABY

It was Mother's Day week-in. Pam's family spent that day alone with her in and out of consciousness. Charlie brought Momma so that we all could spend Mother's Day with her. We gathered at Janice's. We brought covered dishes, and all of Momma's children, grandchildren, and great-grandchildren were there.

Monday morning, Charlie came over to Pam's house before they left to go back to Atlanta. Momma knew that Pam might not wake up since she was in and out of consciousness. We gathered around the bed.

"Pam, Momma is here."

She opened her eyes and tried to lift herself, reaching her arms out toward Momma like a little girl reaching for her mommy. She said softly, "Momma."

Pam's daughters got in the bed with her and sat behind her. They lifted her from behind so that she could sit up. Pam wanted to touch Momma.

Charlie pushed Momma's wheelchair over to the side of the bed. He pushed her footrest to the side, placing her feet on the floor, and stood Momma straight up. Her full body weight was against him as he stood behind her.

Jimmy moved the wheelchair out of the way. We moved Pam's legs off to the side of the bed so that they could face each other. Pam reached out toward Momma and wrapped her arms around Momma's neck. She whispered, "Momma, I don't want this to hurt you."

Plastic Tulips in the Winter

Momma cried out from deep in her soul, "My baby, my baby, my baby." Pam's tears fell on Mom's neck as she held her tight.

Pam whispered, "Momma... I love you." She laid her face against Momma's neck the way a baby does its mother.

Momma responded, "I love you; I love you; I love you; you are my baby."

We were all crying as we laid Pam back down, and she fell into a deep sleep.

We went into the living room and decided it would be better for Charlie to take Momma back to Atlanta, where she had all her necessities. We told him we'd keep him informed and would call if we saw a turning towards the end. Momma must rest for the days that lay ahead.

Denice Vickers

38

Run Toward The Light

THE NEXT DAY, all of Pam's family was in and out of the bedroom, taking turns sitting with her. Janice crawled up into the bed with her, loved on her, saying, "You have been the most wonderful sister to me. You have loved me so beautifully. I always knew you loved me, Pam."

Leeann was holding Pam's feet, saying, "My darling Angel." Tears ran down Leeann's cheek.

I took my turn with her. I lay across her body and cried. Her eyes were now open, but she was not blinking, and her breathing was slow and shallow. Her eyes fixed, and we knew today would be the day we would say goodbye.

All the family, except the youngest grandchildren, stood around Pam's bed. Janice and I were at the foot of the bed. Janice was kneeling, and I was standing next to her. Pam's children and their spouses were on each side of the bed. My children and their spouses were in the room, also. Steve was standing next to me.

It would take Charlie about two hours to get Momma fed, bathed, dressed, and on the road toward Montgomery. We told him to go ahead and get on the interstate and come. Her breathing was changing. It was slow as she gasped for air. We didn't want to see her struggle for breath. I felt she was waiting for us to release her and let her go. I knew Momma wasn't there, but I also knew Momma would not want her baby struggling for air.

I looked down at Janice, and in a firm direct tone, "Janice, tell Pam to run toward the light." Janice cut her eyes toward me, "No."

Holding back tears, again, "Janice, you tell Pam to run toward the light."

Janice looked at me, paused, and took a deep breath as she gave the command, "Pam," she paused, "Run toward the light. Run!"

I then yelled, "Go, Pam! Run! Pam, run to the light! Go to Jesus! Go into His arms! Cross over, Pam!" Everyone in the room began to say, "Go to Jesus! Run to His arms."

Plastic Tulips in the Winter

I yelled again, "Pam, cross over! Run, Pam! Run toward the light!"

Right then, Pam took three deep breaths. Chill bumps appeared all over her arms, and then she was gone. She exhaled her last breath, and we could see her spirit leave her body. It was the most beautiful sight I have ever seen. It was powerful, it was mighty, it was holy, and the Holy of Holies was in the room. It was more beautiful than the birth of a newborn baby.

The Hospice nurses waited in the other room, allowing us to have these last moments with our precious sister. They said they had never experienced a family so beautifully sending off a loved one. We asked them not to take her until our mother arrived. They waited for three hours. The hearse was out front waiting, and a police officer came and stood in the corner of the bedroom by the fireplace, very respectfully, like a soldier protecting royalty.

The phone rang in the kitchen, and Leeann answered it. It was Daddy. "This is Charles Perkins. How is Pam doing?"

Ten months and he had finally called and wanted to know about his child. His black and white picture was still next to her bed on her nightstand. She loved to be held by Daddy. "Hold me, Daddy. Hold me." He never called to check on her during the ten months she was getting chemo. But still, she kept his photo there beside her bed to remember to pray for him. Now he calls, he calls to late.

Leeann said, "Well, Daddy, it's odd you called, she just passed away an hour ago."

"She did?" Then his song and dance routine began. "Well, I'm not going to be able to come to the funeral. I haven't been feeling well."

He didn't skip a beat and immediately gave his excuse as to why he would not show up for his own child's funeral. My mind, my soul, cannot comprehend such shallow emotion. If I had to crawl and drag my body, I would be there for my child.

Leeann said, "You son of a bitch," and hung up. I thought, "How strange he called right after she took her last breath."

I called Charlie on his cell phone. "Charlie, Pam just passed away." The words were hard to say. "She's gone."

He, Jimmy, and Momma were already in the car driving on the interstate heading toward Montgomery. I heard him say, "Momma, Pam is gone."

Plastic Tulips in the Winter

Momma cried out from the depth of her soul with a deep moan. I heard her say, "I want to stop all these cars and tell them, my baby just passed away, that my baby is in the presence of God. They don't know what just happened to my baby. These people don't realize today is not just another day. My baby, my baby! Oh, my baby," she cried. I felt her pain. The world doesn't stop when we are in pain. The heart just keeps on beating.

I hung the phone up, looked at Janice, as our eyes met, "We did good."

She nodded and said back to me, "We did good."

We both knew what we were referring to. We let Pam wrap her arms and legs around us so that she would feel safe. We did that for her again as she took her final journey. We did good.

Charlie arrived with Momma. He brought her into the room in her wheelchair to see her baby one last time before they took her body away.

Momma's body was slumped forward in her wheelchair as if she could hardly breathe. Her eyes looked at her child with such sadness and pain. I wondered how her body could hold up under such pain in her soul. She raised her head and hand toward God, and for the second time in my life, I saw her ball her fist up in the air and say, "My baby." Momma wept.

Pam's body was wheeled outside on a gurney with a sheet covering her. I stood on the front porch of Pam's house. They placed her in the hearse and shut the doors. The hearse took a right turn out of the driveway. It was a dead-end street, so it passed by the house again before leaving the neighborhood. I didn't like the thought of her body being in the back of that hearse alone.

I whispered under my breath, "Bye Pam, I love you. I will miss you." My soul longed for her to stay. I watched as the hearse left her street, it disappeared.

THE FUNERAL

My sister had died, and it was time for Steve and me to be her pastor. We prepared for the funeral. The church was packed. Pam's children each shared a story about their mother. She would have been so proud of them.

I shared the events about Pam's life—the eight boxes of Valentine candy, the day she defended me, and I fought Fat Henrietta with my frog. I told them, "Pam is looking down at me right now, laughing. I feel her." I shared she was my biggest cheerleader in life, always bragging about me to others, and telling me the message I taught helped her. Every time I preached at the church, Pam ordered at least eight tapes of my sermon and passed them around town. I told them, Pam and I had lived together while our spouses were in the Navy. That Pam and I ran after God together.

I told them how I tried to get Pam to flirt with her boss to get him to notice her. The congregation laughed and cried. I continued, "It was an honor to have been blessed with my sister. I have been lucky in life to love her the way I did, and to be loved by her." Then I ended by saying, "She is not in my past. She is in my future. I will see her again."

Her death was spiritual, beautiful— it was personal, painful, empty, and I miss her. Pam passed away Wednesday, May 11, 2005. She was fifty-six years old.

After everything was over, I crashed. The grief was unbearable. I woke up, and my first thought was, this can't be true. Pam came to me in my dreams, always smiling, and I would ask, "Why are you here? You died." She just continued smiling at me.

Janice started staying at her beach house in Destin, Florida. She just didn't want to be in Montgomery with all the reminders of Pam. We tried going into department stores, and the salespeople would ask, "Where is the other sister?" It was too painful to say she passed away. Janice just couldn't do it any longer.

I told Steve I needed a break from the ministry. I felt I had nothing left to give. The wound to my soul, the separation between earth, and heaven at first was unbelievable pain. The heart does not have a calendar when it comes to grief, it just keeps beating. You keep breathing, but the pain remains. There are no words that can-do justice for this moment in one's life. Death knocks on everyone's door eventually. Your prayer will be, "Oh God, help me take my next breath."

I kept telling God, I missed her. He answered back, "She doesn't miss you."

When I accepted the fact that I missed Pam, but she did not miss me, I began to heal. I know for Pam; it will be as if it was a few seconds ago when we last saw each other. This is a part of life for everyone. We do not learn this through books but experience. Life is a teacher, isn't it?

THE BANQUET TABLE

Little Denice's marriage ended in divorce with no children after four years. Our son Stephen and his wife Hillary were moving to Los Angeles to pursue his career as a singer and songwriter. We decided to go too. After twenty-six years of pastoring, we turned the church over to our oldest daughter, Stacy, and her husband, Brian.

Plastic Tulips in the Winter

We kept our home in Montgomery and leased a beautiful home in the hills of LA, California. I could see the Hollywood sign from my back yard.

We left our home in Montgomery furnished so that we could come back and forth from LA. That way, we could see our children and grandchildren and spend time with Momma, who was still with Charlie and Jimmy.

On one visit to Atlanta to see Mom, she told me, "Denice, something happened last night. I don't know if I saw it or if it was a dream. It seemed so real."

I told her to tell me about it. "I stepped into this room in heaven, and I saw a beautiful banquet table with people sitting at it. Denice, the table was breathtaking. Pam was sitting there, talking, and laughing. When she saw me, she waved for me to come and sit across from her. Pam had saved me a seat. She was so excited to see me, and it was as if she heard I was coming, and they were all waiting for me. She pointed at the empty seat."

I said, "Momma, I believe that was from God. Maybe you're fixing to go join Pam."

With excitement, "That would be wonderful. Perhaps so!"

I told her, "Momma, I believe Pam is saving you a seat."

"I do too," in such a tender voice, and a look of peace and excitement in her eyes.

It was getting harder and harder for Charlie to take care of Momma, and we all agreed she should be in a nursing home in Montgomery. I stayed to help Charlie get her settled in a nursing home near my house. I ate lunch with her and got to know each person at her table. She and two others in their wheelchairs became buddies. Every day I took them outside to the gazebo and read a book to them.

Leeann told the owner that she would give the cafeteria a full face-lift — a total make-over at no expense to the nursing home. Momma was so proud of Leeann and how talented she was.

She lived for five more weeks. It was a blessing that I got to be with her during those weeks. It was Easter Sunday weekend. The nurse in the nursing home tried to wake mom, but she had had another stroke. We filled the hospital room with family, taking turns loving on Momma, singing all the church songs that had meant so much to her.

Realizing Pam wasn't there to take Momma's last breath. I sat on the edge of her bed. I pressed my lips against her lips, letting her breath into my mouth. I breathed in her breath. I looked over at Janice and winked. She smiled and said, "I know what you're doing."

I smiled at her with a twinkle in my eye and said, "I told you and Pam, I would be the one." I kissed her face and told her I loved her "Momma," repeatedly. "Momma, Momma," kissing her lips. It was such a beautiful word to me, "Momma."

Momma passed away on April 9th, 2007. I know Pam was sitting at that banquet table in heaven — having gotten word that Momma was coming. She was smiling, waving for Mom to join her. Pam had saved Momma a seat.

39

Green Valley Funeral Home

WE RECEIVED WORD Daddy was in a nursing home in Birmingham, Alabama. Charlie and Leeann went to see him twice. Daddy had always said he wasn't Charlie's daddy. Charlie wanted to know, one way or another. Charlie and Leeann told Daddy they were going to check his dentures. Charlie ordered a DNA test kit. He swabbed Daddy's mouth, sent the kit off, and got the results a few days later. The test came back ninety-nine percent positive Daddy was Charlie's father.

One afternoon, Leeann called. She said, "I received a phone call this morning from a funeral director at Green Valley Funeral Home near Birmingham. He said he had Daddy's body and asked if we wanted to view it. The director felt someone should view it before lowered into the ground."

I told Lee, "I'll go if you're busy with your store's grand opening. Don't feel guilty for not going. You know Leeann, if you had died, he wouldn't have bothered coming."

"Let me think about it overnight."

Charlie and Jimmy were out of the country for a month traveling around Morocco. They were to arrive home that Wednesday. Janice, Leeann, Steve, and I went together.

We arrived at the funeral home. The director walked us into a conference room. We sat down, and he opened a folder. "Your father had come by a few years ago to take care of the arrangements. He did not want a service or a viewing, just put in the ground. Two women dropped by with a death certificate, but they did not want to view him. What are your wishes?"

We all agreed we needed a moment with Daddy. The director said that Daddy was not in a coffin but would be on a table with a sheet covering all but his neck and head.

He led us into a room, and there he lay. Daddy looked as he did the last time. He looked like an older man that could have been a loving father, maybe a man who loved his children and grandchildren. He could have been a man that had been successful in his life—

one who's loved ones wept at his passing. The reality was, no one was weeping, and no one came, but the children he turned his back on.

We stood silently, looking down at his lifeless body on the table. The director stood in the back of the room as he heard me speak up.

"Well, Daddy, here we are. You know, you never did right with your children. You never loved us. You missed out; we were great kids. We are good people. Your life was a sad life. You know, Daddy, everyone liked you. Nobody loved you, except those you walked away from, Momma, and your kids. It was all about money, and what your flesh wanted. Now you're gone. You are dead, and none of those things you loved more than family are with you. I choose to close the last page of this chapter in my life. I do not need you. I have all I need in this life to make me complete. Your children are blessed. We have found love without you."

Janice was standing to the right of me. She spoke sincerely, and with mercy, but trembling, "I don't know if you are in heaven or hell, but I believe you can hear me wherever you are. I know you had mental problems, so I forgive you for being a child molester." She took a few steps back. That's all she had to say. It was enough.

Leeann began to sob. I pulled her close to me and held her. "I have no childhood memory of Daddy," she said. I whispered in her ear, "I know."

ONE DOLLAR

The next morning, I called the woman who had his death certificate. "Your daddy always said you, kids, didn't belong to him."

I could tell by the tone in her voice he had talked bad about us. At that point, I didn't care to change her thoughts. I just simply said,

"Yeah, it was his way of not having any guilt about abandoning us."

She spoke up, "Well, in his will, he did leave you kids, something." She spoke in a way, which told me dad had told her all we wanted was his money.

She continued, "He left each child a one-dollar bill." That was a slap in the face from Daddy.

She continued, "Your daddy always went to the nursing home chapel service, and he loved his gospel music."

"Yeah, he always did love those quartets," I responded.

All my life, I felt that in the end, Daddy would make it into heaven. Not by his own right, but by the mercy of God, and the prayers of Momma, and his children. Who knows the thoughts of a person taking his last breath? If he did make it into heaven, I'm sure the pearly gates kicked him in the butt, as he entered.

I called Leeann, and Janice to tell them of their one-dollar inheritance. The two women got his home and everything in it, including his car.

Janice answered, "Well, he can take it to his grave because that is the only thing he loved in his life — money."

We were still waiting for Charlie to arrive back in the States. Charlie called from Atlanta. We agreed that Janice and I would meet him and Jimmy at the funeral home the next morning so Charlie could have closure.

Janice and I sat in the waiting room, finishing our Starbucks before they arrived.

Charlie and Jimmy walked in, and we hugged each other, talked about their overseas trip. The director walked up, asked if we were ready to view Daddy's body.

In the room was a baby blue coffin. Dad was wearing a beige suit, a starched cream dress shirt, and a baby blue tie. Charlie, Janice, and I stood looking down at Daddy.

Charlie spoke up in a trembling voice, "Daddy, I forgive you for molesting me, and for grooming me to be molested. I was young and wanted so badly to have a daddy. I wanted you to love me. You told me that you wanted to show me a gun you had in your suitcase. You held it in your hand and said for me not to tell Momma about it. You said it was a secret between us, between buddies, that men have secrets together. Then you took advantage of me, a child. I realize now that you didn't have it in you to love me. I truly forgive you; I hope you're at peace, and I hope God had mercy on your soul. The times that I did see you, I thought you had a good personality. You were funny in a strange kind of way. Everybody around you seemed to like you. I would have liked you if I hadn't known what I knew about you."

Charlie laughed as he looked down at Daddy to make one last statement, "Your dick and money are all you cared about."

I laughed, "On that note, Daddy, you left each of your children one dollar. We do not want to inherit anything from you. So, here are five one-dollar bills from all of us. One is from Pam. We want you to take it with you to your grave. We do not need anything from you."

Plastic Tulips in the Winter

Charlie tucked the five one-dollar bills into Daddy's suit. Janice and I walked over to sit down with Jimmy and left Charlie looking down at Daddy.

Charlie said to Dad, "Well, speak up. Don't you have anything to say for yourself?"

We all laughed. Charlie walked over to us, lit a cigarette, smoked a few puffs off it, and flicked the butt in the coffin with Daddy.

I gasped for breath, and exclaimed, "Charlie, he is embalmed! His body could explode with fire!"

We burst out in laughter. I know it sounds disrespectful the way we laughed, but I also realized it was because we were truly free from the pain he had caused in our lives. We were not his victims. We were like what the Bible promises His children, "Above, and not beneath, the head, and not the tail."

Charlie lifted the lid of the part of the coffin that was closed over Daddy's legs and feet. There was a plastic bag between his legs that held his false teeth, his wallet, a paperback Gideon Bible, and his cheap watch. Charlie opened the wallet. There was a one-dollar bill in it.

Charlie asked, "I wonder why he had a one-dollar bill in his wallet?"

"Maybe he wanted to give it to Pam when he got to heaven," I responded; we laughed.

The director walked in to say they were ready to put him in the ground. We drove our cars to the gravesite and arrived just as the hearse pulled up. It was dead of winter, frost was on the ground, and the sky was overcast. A damp, cold breeze was blowing. We bundled up with our sweaters and coats to get warm. The director, two older men, and a young man in his twenties set the coffin down onto the belts to lower it into the ground. No one else was there to testify to a life lived only the children that he said we're no good and did not belong to him.

Charlie walked over and lifted the lid of the coffin to look one last time. In all my years in the ministry, I have never seen anyone open the coffin at the gravesite.

I looked at the director to see his response to Charlie opening the lid. He seemed to make a quick decision, allowing him to do what he needed for closure. The director had overheard everything. Charlie began to lower the lid, and the director reached to give a helping hand. Charlie pushed his hand away as if to say; I need to be the one to do this. Then he slammed it shut. Charlie then walked around to the other side of the casket. They began to lower it into the ground, and Charlie then kicked the coffin as hard as he could.

A feeling of victory swept over me as I saw him do that. I no longer saw a passive boy; I saw a strong man. I had the thought; "The young boy became a man and kicked the loser's coffin." He then walked over to stand by Janice and me. Trembling, he said, "I'm sorry."

I quickly responded, "You have the right to do and say anything you feel at this moment. It is our closure. I'm proud of you as a man, and I'm proud of all Momma's kids. We are good people. Our Momma loved us, and her love was enough."

We watched his coffin as it lowered into the ground. Janice, Charlie, Jimmy, and I gave a group hug to say goodbye to each other and then turned and walked to our cars.

I opened the door to my red Lexus convertible and paused for one last look toward his grave.

I suddenly noticed all the plastic roses left at every headstone. How strange, I thought, "Daddy spent his whole life surrounding himself with plastic things, and now in death, he will spend all of eternity buried among all the plastic flowers. How fitting.

One day I might come by and put some plastic tulips on his grave. I'll push them in the ground, and he will have plastic tulips in the winter. He would like that. Isn't it something, I still care.

Just as he had said in the past, "When people drive by and see them, they will wonder how Tulips can grow in the winter." His grave will be the only one that can grow plastic tulips in the winter."

40

Ashes To Ashes, Dust To Dust

Summer 2007

ASHES TO ASHES, dust to dust. Momma always said she wanted a marching band with a choir singing "When the Saints Go Marching In." She wanted it to be a time of celebration.

There, Janice and I stood. She was sixty, and I was not far behind. Oh, where did the years go?

As Janice and I looked out over the ocean, the setting sun cast an orange hue across the water. All the sunbathers and the children playing had gone in for the evening.

Our toes were dug deep into the wet sand as the waves rushed over our feet. The breeze, filled with the salty air, blew against our faces. We stood side by side, looking in deep silence, and from the depths of my being, I heard my soul cry, "Momma, are we there yet?"

Our eyes were fixed on Steve, and Tom as they stood waist-deep in the water, slowly sprinkling Momma's ashes from two clear plastic bags.

Steve was now in his sixties and still very handsome and distinguished, looking with white hair and a mustache.

I thought of all the people who were enjoying the beach that day. They had no idea someone's ashes were being scattered in the sea, someone whose life counted so much.

There was no choir or marching band, no celebration. The breeze blew Momma's ashes as they skipped across the top of the blue water. I whispered, "Momma." That was such a beautiful word to me.

I gave her a queen's wave, "Bye, Momma. Go into the ocean that you loved. It always brought you such peace."

I took a deep breath as a thousand memories flooded my mind. I began to answer my own question, "Momma are we there yet?"

Plastic Tulips in the Winter

"Momma, I now understand that the journey through life is the destination. We were always there."

"Momma, you taught me that life is more than plastic tulips. When the storms came with all its sorrow, and tears, we hunkered down, and trusted God, knowing the sun would shine again. We laughed and danced for joy with the taste of victory in our mouths. It was part of our journey through this life. You taught me to hope in God. God is the answer."

"I now know that the test of life comes to us all, and bad things happen to good people. I will never give up; I will always try one more time. I've learned that the powerful weapon of choice that has been given to us all, determines how we go through life."

"Mom, I choose to dance in the sun, and I will dance in the rain."

"I realize money will be made, and money will be lost. Children and grandchildren will marry and divorce. Babies will be born and loved ones will die."

"You have taught me how to live and love life with all its obstacles. Life happens to us all, and we determine the journey. Life, at its best, is beautiful — full of love and laughter. But even at life's lowest moments, life is still worth living."

"God, laughter, and tears intertwined the hearts and souls of you and your children. It gave us the strength to fight life through this glorious journey called Life."

Mom, with the help of God, I will find a new normal in life's journey without you and Pam until I see you both again at the banquet table. *"Save me a seat."*

A story told is a life lived. This is my story.

Denice Vickers

Acknowledgments

I would like to acknowledge the following people; whose encouragement and support have been invaluable to me in the writing of this book:

First, and foremost, my husband Steve, and our children, Stacy, Misty, Stephen, and Denice, who believed I had something to say, and never lost faith in me.

Janice, my sister, got tired of me asking her, "Is the book good." She finally told me not to ask her again. Thanks for believing in me.

Thank you to James Thayer, Migdalia Pabon, Colleen Cady, and Irma Alexander, who was the best friend's life could have given. They believed in me.

My special thanks go to all the sweet people of Montgomery, Alabama, past, and present.

Again, thank you to my son, Stephen, who designed this book cover.

Steve, and I now live in Palm Springs, California

Visit me online: www.denicevickers.com